The Work Sampling System.

Teacher's Manual

The Work Sampling System is a performance assessment that provides an alternative to group-administered, norm-referenced achievement tests in preschool through fifth grade. Its purpose is to document and assess children's skills, knowledge, behavior, and accomplishments across a wide variety of curriculum areas on multiple occasions.

The Work Sampling System consists of three complementary elements:

1) Developmental Guidelines and Checklists,
2) Portfolios of children's work, and
3) Summary Reports.

Assessments based on the Work Sampling approach take place three times a year. They are designed to reflect classroom goals and objectives and to help teachers keep track of children's continuous progress by placing their work within a broad, developmental perspective. Through its focus on documenting individual performance of classroom-based tasks, Work Sampling enhances student motivation, assists teachers in instructional decision-making, and serves as an effective means for reporting children's progress to families, professional educators, and the community.

Teacher's Manual

Margo L. Dichtelmiller
Judy R. Jablon
Aviva B. Dorfman
Dorothea B. Marsden
Samuel J. Meisels

The Work Sampling System®

REBUS PLANNING ASSOCIATES, INC.
ANN ARBOR, MICHIGAN

For more information about
The Work Sampling System, write to:
Rebus Planning Associates, Inc.
1103 South University Avenue
Ann Arbor, Michigan 48104

Preparation of this document was supported in part by a grant from the John D. and Catherine T. MacArthur Foundation. The opinions expressed are solely those of the authors.

DESIGNED AND PRODUCED BY MODE DESIGN.

Printed in the United States of America.

96 95   10 9 8 7 6 5 4 3

Part No. 30011 (2/95)
ISBN 1-57212-102-5

Contents

CHAPTER 5
Special Topics

Contents

List of Frequently Asked Questions

CHAPTER 4
Summary Reports

List of Work Sampling System Materials

Introductory descriptions, in most cases followed by an illustration, for the following Work Sampling System materials can be found on the pages indicated:

Foreword

THE WORK SAMPLING SYSTEM HAS ITS ORIGINS IN THE KINDERGARTEN classroom where I first started teaching in 1970. This was an exciting time to teach young children. Head Start was still in its infancy, Piaget had just been "rediscovered," and open classrooms were capturing the imagination of teachers everywhere. The classroom I designed at the Runkle School in Brookline, Massachusetts was rich in the possibilities of learning. It had climbing structures, books, balance beams, aquaria filled with fish, reptiles, and small mammals, a nest of rabbits with their young, books and counting objects, blocks, a carpenter's bench, extensive art materials, and children's work everywhere. With a very specific set of purposes in mind, I set out to create a highly active learning environment. It was one that would allow me to teach children about themselves and their world while informing me about how they were learning so that I could enhance and extend their development. The classroom I designed in 1970 and the following year when I took on a combination kindergarten/first grade sought to meet these goals. They were settings that afforded children a multitude of opportunities to explore their world. My interactions with students helped me set individual goals for children, making use of the extensive learning potential implicit in the classroom environment.

However, one area resisted all of my best efforts and thinking. How could I evaluate what my students were learning? The testing culture we have grown accustomed to in recent years had not yet reached down to five and six year olds at that time, but the tests that were available seemed to me to be completely inappropriate. I was looking for a way to tell me how *well* my students were doing by documenting *what* my students were doing. Nothing available seemed to answer this need, and my own efforts were not very successful.

The checklists I constructed had no structure or justification beyond my own classroom. The folders of student work that I collected became an experience of information overload, and I could not sustain them past the first few months of school. My reports to parents — although filled with rich anecdotal information — were unsystematic and idiosyncratic.

In succeeding years I carried my quest for a practical and meaningful classroom assessment with me to new settings. After leaving the classroom I became a faculty member at Tufts University and director of the Eliot-Pearson Children's School. The staff at Eliot-Pearson helped me gain some clarity and try out several different approaches to assessment, but the task of creating a useful mechanism for teachers to assess and document their students' classroom accomplishments remained unfinished.

I returned to this challenge again in the mid-80s when controversy began to rage about the inappropriate uses of tests with young children. As a critic of high stakes testing and the role of tests in enrollment and promotion decisions regarding young children, my research at Michigan began to coalesce around the need for assessment alternatives. In 1990 I turned once more to this unfinished task.

With the assistance of several exceptionally gifted colleagues and numerous generous and talented classroom teachers, the Work Sampling System began to take shape. From the outset it had three elements: a checklist, portfolio, and summary report. At first it was intended only to be a kindergarten assessment. Shortly, however, we began to develop preschool versions. This was followed by extensions to grade 3, and finally grade 5. Fundamental to the development of Work Sampling was a process of field trial, reviews by teachers and staff, and revision. This cycle went on as many as five times for some elements of the System. Over a four year period, we held focus groups with teachers, interviewed principals and supervisors, met with consultants, sent out questionnaires, completed a pilot research study, and revised our work extensively. The present version of the Work Sampling System is thus indebted to the hundreds of teachers and other educators who were willing to try to make Work Sampling a useful part of their professional lives and who shared their implementation experiences with us.

It is now nearly 25 years since I first encountered the problem of documenting and evaluating children's classroom accomplishments and learning. One thing I have learned is that there are no easy answers and no simple solutions. Children are too varied and their interactions with the world of other children, adults, and materials are so complex that conventional forced choice assessment solutions are at best unrealistic estimates of the phenomena of growth and development that we are trying to document. The Work Sampling System is a means for capturing these phenomena. It does not stand on its own: it comes to life only in the hands of a teacher. Like a car it needs a driver, like a book it requires a reader, like a musical composition it calls for a performer. The Work Sampling System is a tool for teachers. It is carefully designed so that it relies on the best knowledge available, provides extensive information to parents and administrators, and captures children's knowledge, skills, and accomplishments as fully and reliably as possible. Work Sampling helps teachers keep track of their students' accomplishments in the world of learning. It makes visible the processes and products that are part of daily classroom life, thus providing teachers with the information they need to create responsive educational experiences for all of their students.

Like teaching itself, Work Sampling is constantly evolving for its developers and users. This Manual is designed to open new possibilities to teachers. I invite you to study this manual, learn about Work Sampling's potential, and discover how this approach to performance assessment can add to your insight and effectiveness as a classroom teacher.

— *Samuel J. Meisels*

Ann Arbor, Michigan
July 1994

How to Use This Book

THIS MANUAL IS INTENDED FOR TEACHERS WHO ARE IMPLEMENTING the Work Sampling System and for those interested in learning more about it. The book is divided into six chapters and appendixes, including a glossary. Chapter 1 provides an overview of the Work Sampling System and a perspective on performance assessment. Chapters 2 – 4 treat the three elements of the System — Developmental Guidelines and Checklists, Portfolios, and Summary Reports. Chapter 5 discusses a number of issues that are central to Work Sampling, such as working with specialists, special needs students, and approaches to involving families and the community. The final chapter reviews ways of getting started with Work Sampling.

Structure of the Chapters

Each of the chapters that focuses on the Work Sampling System elements has a common structure intended to help teachers who are implementing Work Sampling. The first sections of each of these chapters provide an overview of the element, definitions of terms, and basic information concerning implementation. The middle section uses a question/answer format to address specific issues that have been raised by teachers who have used Work Sampling in the past. The final section is devoted to a discussion of special topics that relate to the particular elements (e.g., for Guidelines and Checklists, a discussion of observation; for Portfolios, a discussion of age-related differences in portfolio collection; for Summary Reports, a discussion of how to write narrative commentaries).

Using the Manual

We suggest that teachers who are beginning to implement Work Sampling start by reading through the first chapter, the first sections of each of Chapters 2 – 4, and the final chapter. After using Work Sampling for a few weeks we encourage teachers to return to the three middle chapters about the Work Sampling elements and read them completely and more carefully. By this time, some of the issues raised in the special topics chapter will become important for teachers. After scanning the topics covered there, teachers can select those issues that are most relevant to their particular situations.

Working with Colleagues

In writing this book we made extensive use of examples, illustrations, and anecdotes collected from classrooms using Work Sampling. We hope that these materials will help teachers solve problems and come to a better understanding of how to use the Work Sampling System. Although we have provided enough information for teachers to use Work Sampling meaningfully, it is most desirable for teachers to work with other colleagues when implementing Work Sampling. Focused discussions with colleagues are essential for gaining better understanding of the Work Sampling performance indicators, devising common Core Items for portfolios, working out practical concerns about the timing of Summary Reports, developing criteria for evaluation, and deciding how to communicate Work Sampling information to families. More ideas and programs for working with colleagues are available in other staff development materials produced as part of the Work Sampling System.

Beginning Gradually

Above all, in beginning to use the Work Sampling System, start gradually. Work Sampling is a comprehensive assessment system that documents the performance and progress of 3 – 11 year old students in all areas of the curriculum, using multiple sources of information collected continuously and reported three times per year. Many teachers find implementing this System to be challenging. In this Manual we suggest several ways of beginning more slowly, for example, start with only 3 or 4 domains; make the first Summary Report shorter than the last one. Over time Work Sampling will become a part of your thinking about children and a way to help you structure your teaching. This Manual is designed to help you gain these skills over time, just as your students grow and develop throughout the year.

Registering with the Work Sampling System

Enclosed with every Work Sampling System Classroom Pack and Teacher Reference Pack is a return postcard that, when mailed, will register a teacher to receive updates, information about follow-up, and a Work Sampling newsletter. Also available for those who register is information about staff development workshops that are offered periodically throughout the year. If no postcard is available, send your name, address, and a request to be placed on the mailing list to: **The Work Sampling System, P.O. Box 1746, Ann Arbor, MI 48106-1746.**

CHAPTER 1

The Work Sampling System: Authentic Performance Assessment For Preschool – Grade 5

FOR DECADES, ASSESSMENT IN AMERICAN SCHOOLS HAS BEEN DOMInated by group-administered, norm-referenced, multiple-choice achievement tests. These tests have held the power to change how teachers and students view themselves and their role in the educational process. But recent research and practice have shown that these tests do more harm than good. They narrow the curriculum. They reduce student motivation to learn. They stigmatize low-achieving students. They give parents very little information about their children's accomplishments. And they shift the focus of the educational process from what is taught in classrooms to an examination of the data that can be used for accountability.

The Work Sampling System replaces the potentially misleading, out-of-context information obtained from conventional readiness and achievement tests with rich, dynamic data about how children respond to real classroom tasks and actual life situations. Work Sampling offers a comprehensive means of monitoring children's social, emotional, physical, and academic progress. It is an authentic *performance assessment* * that is based on teachers' observations of students actively working and creating products within the context of their daily classroom experience.

The advantages of the Work Sampling System are many:

■ It enhances student motivation by emphasizing what children *can* do as contrasted to what they *cannot* do, and by involving students in the process of assessment.

■ It helps teachers gain perspective on how their students learn by evaluating and documenting all areas of growth and development and many diverse learning styles.

■ It is an effective means of reporting children's progress to families because it captures information that is specific to the child, and that is familiar and meaningful to the family.

■ It accommodates a wide range of children, including those with special needs and those from diverse cultural and socio-economic backgrounds.

---

* See the Glossary in Appendix D for definitions of terms shown in ***bold-italic.***

■ It is based on national standards of curriculum development from age 3 to grade 5, relying on three overlapping forms of documentation that give teachers a common language and shared criteria for assessment and collaboration with other teachers, administrators, and families.

Designed for students in preschool through fifth grade, the Work Sampling System consists of three interrelated elements:

■ *Developmental Guidelines* and *Checklists*

■ *Portfolios*

■ *Summary Reports*

These elements are all classroom-focused and instructionally relevant, reflecting the objectives of the classroom teacher. Instead of providing a mere snapshot of narrow academic skills at a single point in time, the Work Sampling System is an ongoing evaluation process designed to improve the teacher's instructional practices and the student's learning.

The continuous assessment format of the Work Sampling System has several important benefits. First, teachers and families can gain perspective on the development of skills and accomplishments over an eight-year period. Second, schools that are committed to mixed age groupings, K – 3 Early Childhood Units, or establishing a unified approach to the elementary curriculum will now be able to use the same assessment over a pupil's entire preschool and elementary career. Third, demonstration projects that must show the year-to-year progress of their students will be able to do so via the longitudinal design of the Work Sampling System. Fourth, because the System addresses a wide range of skills and abilities, the progress of diverse students can be monitored within the same approach. Finally, the Work Sampling System demystifies assessment. It makes easily understood information available to all participants in the teaching/assessment process — children, families, teachers, and administrators. This minimizes the risk of assessments being used to track, label, isolate, or harm individuals or groups of children.

Figure 1 shows the principal elements of the Work Sampling System and illustrates several fundamental features of the System: seven *domains*, or categories, of classroom learning (e.g, Personal and Social Development, Language and Literacy, etc.) and their use throughout the System; three documentation elements (Checklists, Portfolios, Summary Reports); three *collection periods* (Fall, Winter, Spring); the involvement of teachers, students, and families; and the eight age/grade levels available (Preschool-3 – Fifth Grade).

FIGURE 1
Diagrammatic overview of
the Work Sampling System

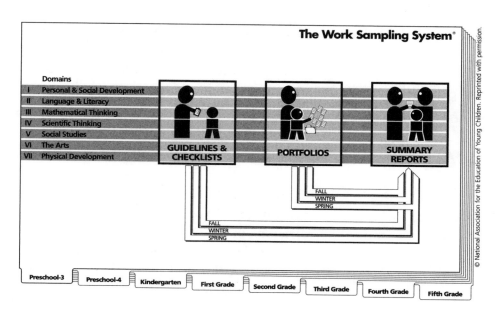

Performance Assessment in the Work Sampling System

Performance assessments are designed to document children's daily activities, provide a means of evaluating the quality of their work, and be flexible enough to take an individualized approach to academic achievement. They are also designed to evaluate abilities that conventional standardized tests do not capture very well. Children are active constructors of knowledge. This means that they are capable of analyzing, synthesizing, evaluating, and interpreting facts and ideas. Performance assessments that focus on classroom activities allow teachers to learn about these processes by documenting how children interact with materials and peers in real-life, "authentic" situations.

All performance assessments require that students demonstrate specific skills and competencies, and that they apply the skills and knowledge they have mastered. The Work Sampling System is an authentic performance assessment, one which focuses on the context in which the student is asked to perform. Therefore, the context must be a "real-life" context, one in which students perform chosen tasks as they would in the process of general instruction.

The Work Sampling System is comprehensive in design. It goes well beyond the many performance assessments that try to assess student competence by exposing children to "on-demand" performance tasks in which choices are severely restricted for both students and teachers. Competence in the Work Sampling System is not assessed on the basis of a single performance. Rather, a student's work is assessed repeatedly through Guidelines and Checklists, teacher observations, and a structured Portfolio. Over time and in the context of numerous performances, teachers can observe the patterns of student learning — what their strengths are, and where their weaker areas might be. These patterns constitute the evidence on which the evaluation is based. Comparisons between students are minimized, since students are evaluated according to how their level of performance conforms to the standards that are built into the Work Sampling System.

Comparisons of a student's performance to a norm are often counterproductive to student motivation and uninformative about the student's capabilities. Rather than producing assessments that are the same for everyone, the Work Sampling System is intended to be sensitive to the different instructional, cultural, social, and personal backgrounds of individual students. It enables teachers to follow children's development over time, within and across domains, in order to create rich profiles or portraits of children's accomplishments and approaches to learning.

The Work Sampling Domains

The Work Sampling System is based on seven categories, or domains, of classroom learning and experience, each of which is carried across all three elements of the System. The seven domains are:

I. Personal and Social Development. This domain has a dual focus. First, it refers to children's feelings about themselves. The teacher can learn about these feelings by observing children, listening to their comments, and hearing families talk about their children. Included in this focus are indicators that refer to children's views of themselves as learners, and their sense of responsibility to themselves and others. The second focus concerns children's social development, including their interactions with peers and adults. Particularly important to this domain are the skills children show they are acquiring while making friends, resolving conflicts, and functioning effectively in groups.

II. Language and Literacy. This domain emphasizes the acquisition of language skills to convey and interpret meaning. All of the components integrate multiple skills, rather than isolated abilities. The indicators in this domain reflect the belief that children learn to read and write the same way they learn to speak — naturally and slowly, using increasingly accurate approximations of adult norms.

III. Mathematical Thinking. Mathematics concerns patterns and relationships, and seeking multiple solutions to problems. The focus of this domain is on children's approaches to mathematical thinking and problem solving. Emphasis is placed on how students acquire and use strategies to perceive, understand, and act on mathematical problems. The content of mathematics (concepts and procedures) is stressed, but within the larger context of understanding and application (knowing and doing).

IV. Scientific Thinking. This domain addresses ways of thinking and inquiring about the natural and physical world. Emphasized are the processes of scientific investigation, because process skills are embedded in and fundamental to all science instruction and content. The focus of this domain is on how children actively investigate through observing, recording, describing, questioning, forming explanations, and drawing conclusions.

V. Social Studies. This domain emphasizes the acquisition of social and cultural understanding. Children acquire this understanding from personal experience and by learning about the experiences of others. As children study present day and historical topics, they gain understanding of human interdependence and the relationships between people and the environment.

VI. The Arts. The emphasis in this domain is on children's engagement with the arts (dance, dramatics, music, and art), both actively and receptively. The components address how children use the arts to express, represent, and integrate their experiences, ideas, and emotions, and how children develop an appreciation for the arts. Rather than emphasizing mastery of skills related to particular art forms, this domain focuses on how using and appreciating the arts enables children to demonstrate what they know and to expand their thinking.

VII. Physical Development. The emphasis in this domain is on physical development as an integral part of children's well-being and ability to take advantage of educational opportunities. The components address gross motor skills, fine motor skills, and personal health and safety. A principal focus is on children's ability to move in ways that demonstrate control, balance, and coordination. Fine motor skills are equally important in laying the groundwork for artistic expression, handwriting, and self-care skills. Also included is children's growing competence to understand and manage their personal health and safety.

Observing, Collecting, and Summarizing

The purpose of the Work Sampling System is to document and assess children's skills, knowledge, behavior, and accomplishments across a wide variety of classroom activities and areas of learning on multiple occasions. It consists of three complementary elements: 1) observations by teachers using Developmental Guidelines and Checklists, 2) collection of children's work in Portfolios, and 3) summaries of this information on Summary Reports.

One of the Work Sampling System's strengths is its systematic structure. It is based on collecting extensive information from multiple sources, and using all of this information collectively to make evaluative decisions about what children know and can do. In its reliance on *observing, collecting,* and *summarizing,* Work Sampling organizes the assessment process so that it is both comprehensive in scope and manageable for teachers and students. Students are observed, information is collected, and performance is summarized on three occasions throughout the school year: fall, winter, and spring. The mechanisms for observing, collecting, and summarizing are as follows:

The **Developmental Guidelines** provide a framework for observation. They give teachers a set of observational criteria that are based on national standards and knowledge of child development. The Guidelines set forth developmentally appropriate expectations for children at each age/grade level. In using the Guidelines as the basis of their professional judgments, teachers in different settings make decisions about children's behavior, knowledge, and accomplishments using identical criteria. Teachers' observations are recorded on the **Developmental Checklists.**

Portfolios are purposeful collections of children's work that illustrate children's efforts, progress, and achievements. These collections are intended to display the individual nature and quality of children's work and progress over time. Work Sampling advocates a structured approach to portfolio collection through the collection of two types of work samples: *Core Items* and *Individualized Items.* Core Items are designed to show growth over time by representing an area of learning within a domain on three occasions during the school year. Individualized Items are designed to portray the unique characteristics of the child and to reflect work that integrates many domains of curriculum. Children and teachers alike are involved in the design, selection, and evaluation of Portfolios.

Summary Reports are completed three times a year. Teachers combine information from the Developmental Checklists and Portfolios with their own knowledge of child development to make evaluative decisions about student performance and progress. They summarize their knowledge of the child as they make ratings and write brief comments describing the student's strengths and areas of concern. Summary Reports take the place of conventional report cards.

Work Sampling not only provides the teacher with clear criteria for evaluation but also incorporates the teacher's expertise and judgment. An evaluation system that does not dictate curriculum or instructional methods, it is designed for use with diverse groups of children, in a variety of settings. The Work Sampling System is a flexible framework for assessment that helps teachers structure their assessments systematically and that encourages teachers to devise techniques best suited to their styles, their students, and their contexts.

Summary

The three elements of the Work Sampling System form an integrated whole. Checklists record a student's growth in relationship to teacher expectations and national standards. Portfolios graphically display the texture and quality of the child's work as well as his or her progress over time. Summary Reports integrate this information into a concise record that the student's family can understand and that administrators can use.

Work Sampling draws upon teachers' perceptions of students while informing, expanding, and structuring their perceptions. It assesses students' development and accomplishments — rather than test-taking skills — in meaningful, curriculum-based activities. It enables children's unique learning styles to be recognized and nurtured, instead of rigidly classifying them as high- or low-achievers based on simplistic assessments. It enables families to become actively involved in the assessment process. And, finally, by objectively documenting what children learn and how teachers teach, the Work Sampling System provides for meaningful evaluation and genuine accountability.

CHAPTER 2

Developmental Guidelines and Checklists

A Structured Approach to Observation, Documentation, and Evaluation

THIS CHAPTER EXAMINES THE WORK SAMPLING SYSTEM GUIDELINES and Checklists. The chapter is divided into five sections:

- Introduction to Developmental Guidelines and Checklists

- The Structure of Guidelines and Checklists

- How to Use Guidelines and Checklists

- Frequently Asked Questions about Guidelines and Checklists

- Further Discussion about Guidelines and Checklists

Introduction to Developmental Guidelines and Checklists

Children engage in many different classroom activities every day. They construct block buildings, participate in class meetings, solve problems, work with manipulatives, talk with their friends, and write in their journals. Teachers observe children as they engage in these learning activities.

Through purposeful and systematic observation of students' behavior, actions, and language, teachers can gather a vast amount of information about children's skills and knowledge. A block structure can show a child's sense of symmetry and balance. Verbal comments during a class meeting may illustrate a child's understanding of human similarities and differences. A child's solution to a math problem may demonstrate the use of several problem solving strategies.

In order for teacher's observations to reflect children's learning accurately, teachers need to know what to look for and how to recognize features of children's learning at different ages. To use observational assessment successfully it is critical that teachers have a framework to help them keep track of their observations. Without such a framework, teachers cannot possibly remember the actions, behaviors, and language of 20 to 30 students for six or eight hours a day. By giving a focus to teacher observations and providing a structure for documentation and evaluation, the Work Sampling System enables teachers to use observational assessment effectively.

The Work Sampling System Guidelines and Checklists guide teachers' reflections about their students, curriculum, and instruction. The Guidelines and Checklists can be used to help teachers focus on students who they do not know very well, and they can serve as a reminder to observe all areas of the curriculum. They can help teachers determine when their instructional plans are working, and when they are not. The common structure of the Guidelines and Checklists for students from three- to eleven-years-old enables teachers to chart children's continuous progress over a wide span of time and development and use this information to plan curricula that reflect individual growth and change.

Fundamentally, Developmental Guidelines and Checklists support teachers in the processes of observation, documentation, and evaluation. The Guidelines focus teacher observations on significant skills, knowledge, and behaviors of children of different ages and provide teachers with developmentally appropriate expectations for their students. They are the lens through which teachers carefully observe children in order to make judgments about their learning and progress. The Checklists enable teachers to document and evaluate students' classroom activities through the use of a detailed profile of a child's knowledge, skills, and behaviors. Together, the Guidelines and Checklists make it possible for teachers to arrive at informed evaluative judgments about student growth and progress after repeated observation and documentation within the context of classroom life.

Description

The Developmental Guidelines provide a systematic framework for evaluating and documenting children's school performance and achievements. They describe reasonable expectations and give detailed rationales and examples for children of different ages across the seven Work Sampling domains. The Guidelines reflect national curriculum standards and child development research. The Developmental Checklist is a tool used to organize and record the observations of student performance that are described in the Guidelines.

Purpose

The purposes of the Guidelines and Checklists are:

1 To give teachers a set of criteria for observation and evaluation that is based on national standards of curriculum development and child development.

2 To focus teacher observations on student acquisition of particular knowledge, skills, and behavior.

3 To help teachers record their observations.

4 To help teachers plan appropriate curriculum and instruction.

Features of Guidelines and Checklists

■ Guidelines and Checklists present each skill, behavior, or accomplishment in the form of a one-sentence *performance indicator*. Each grade level has its own set of 50 – 70 performance indicators.

■ Guidelines elaborate and explain each performance indicator by giving a detailed *rationale* and a set of *examples* or illustrations related to that indicator.

■ Guidelines are available in two formats:

• Grade-level editions of Developmental Guidelines are designed for efficient classroom use with Checklists. Grade-level Guidelines are available in Work Sampling System Classroom Packs and Teacher Reference Packs and include a Wall Chart of Performance Indicators for that grade.

• The *Omnibus Guidelines* presents the Guidelines for six grade levels in a side-by-side format that shows the continuous progress of performance indicators. Recommended for general reference use by teachers and administrators, it is available in two volumes: Vol. 1: Preschool – Third Grade, or Vol. 2: Kindergarten – Fifth Grade.

■ Developmental Checklists contain the performance indicators for a single grade level and allow teachers to rate students on each indicator three times per year.

■ Several observational record forms called Process Notes are available as reproducible black-line masters and are included in Work Sampling Classroom Packs and Teacher Reference Packs.

Structure of Developmental Guidelines and Checklists

The Guidelines and Checklists identify and describe a set of developmentally appropriate skills, knowledge, and behaviors for each age/ grade level across the seven Work Sampling domains. A domain is defined as a broad area of a child's growth and learning. The domains are:

- Personal and Social Development

- Language and Literacy

- Mathematical Thinking

- Scientific Thinking

- Social Studies

- The Arts

- Physical Development

Each domain is comprised of several *functional components* or subsets of the domain. For example, the domain of Mathematical Thinking is composed of these functional components:

- Approach to mathematical thinking

- Patterns and relationships

- Number concept and operations

- Geometry and spatial relationships

- Measurement

- Probability and statistics

Like domains, most functional components appear throughout the eight age/grade levels of the Work Sampling System. However, some components appear only in the levels where they are developmentally appropriate. For example, in the domain of Mathematical Thinking, the last component, probability and statistics, appears only in grades 1 – 5.

Finally, each component is comprised of a set of performance indicators. These presentations of skills, behaviors, attitudes, and accomplishments are the primary focus for teacher observations. Performance indicators are specific to each grade level in the System, but many are similar from grade to grade. Figure 1 shows the relationship between domain, functional components, and performance indicators for Language and Literacy. The performance indicators shown are from the first grade Guidelines.

FIGURE 1

Relationship of domain, functional components, and performance indicators for Language and Literacy, first grade

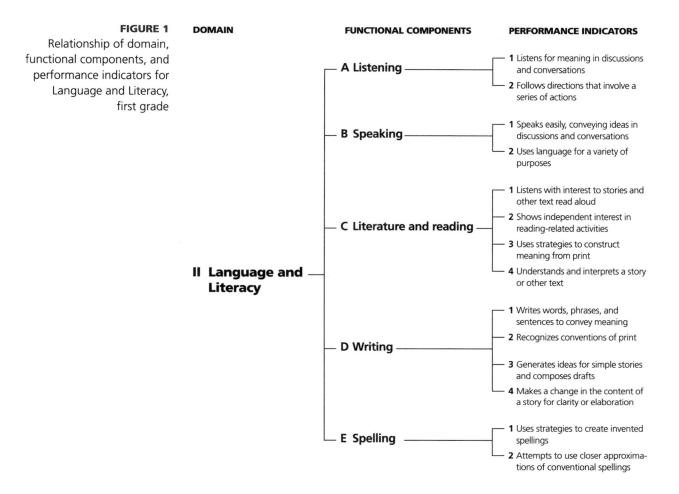

DOMAIN

II **Language and Literacy**

FUNCTIONAL COMPONENTS

A **Listening**

B **Speaking**

C **Literature and reading**

D **Writing**

E **Spelling**

PERFORMANCE INDICATORS

1 Listens for meaning in discussions and conversations

2 Follows directions that involve a series of actions

1 Speaks easily, conveying ideas in discussions and conversations

2 Uses language for a variety of purposes

1 Listens with interest to stories and other text read aloud

2 Shows independent interest in reading-related activities

3 Uses strategies to construct meaning from print

4 Understands and interprets a story or other text

1 Writes words, phrases, and sentences to convey meaning

2 Recognizes conventions of print

3 Generates ideas for simple stories and composes drafts

4 Makes a change in the content of a story for clarity or elaboration

1 Uses strategies to create invented spellings

2 Attempts to use closer approximations of conventional spellings

Grade-level Developmental Guidelines

The Work Sampling System's eight grade-level DEVELOPMENTAL GUIDELINES, from age 3 to grade 5, provide an overall view of what children can be expected to learn each year. The Guidelines elaborate and explain each performance indicator using rationales and examples to describe developmentally appropriate expectations for children's mastery at each age/grade level.

Guidelines are color-coded by grade level (colors match those used on Developmental Checklists)

Domain name and brief description

Components are labeled with letters

Performance indicators are listed numerically after component names (indicator text matches that used on the Checklist)

Each indicator is followed by a detailed rationale that states age level expectations

Each indicator also includes several examples that illustrate some ways children might demonstrate the indicator in daily classroom activities

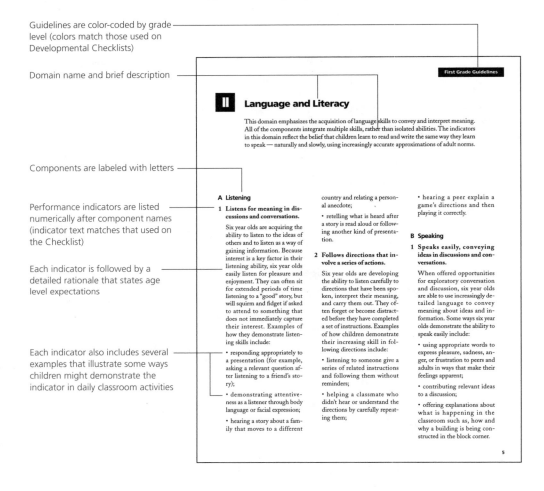

First Grade Guidelines

▐ Language and Literacy

This domain emphasizes the acquisition of language skills to convey and interpret meaning. All of the components integrate multiple skills, rather than isolated abilities. The indicators in this domain reflect the belief that children learn to read and write the same way they learn to speak — naturally and slowly, using increasingly accurate approximations of adult norms.

A Listening

1 Listens for meaning in discussions and conversations.

Six year olds are acquiring the ability to listen to the ideas of others and to listen as a way of gaining information. Because interest is a key factor in their listening ability, six year olds easily listen for pleasure and enjoyment. They can often sit for extended periods of time listening to a "good" story, but will squirm and fidget if asked to attend to something that does not immediately capture their interest. Examples of how they demonstrate listening skills include:

• responding appropriately to a presentation (for example, asking a relevant question after listening to a friend's story);

• demonstrating attentiveness as a listener through body language or facial expression;

• hearing a story about a family that moves to a different country and relating a personal anecdote;

• retelling what is heard after a story is read aloud or following another kind of presentation.

2 Follows directions that involve a series of actions.

Six year olds are developing the ability to listen carefully to directions that have been spoken, interpret their meaning, and carry them out. They often forget or become distracted before they have completed a set of instructions. Examples of how children demonstrate their increasing skill in following directions include:

• listening to someone give a series of related instructions and following them without reminders;

• helping a classmate who didn't hear or understand the directions by carefully repeating them;

• hearing a peer explain a game's directions and then playing it correctly.

B Speaking

1 Speaks easily, conveying ideas in discussions and conversations.

When offered opportunities for exploratory conversation and discussion, six year olds are able to use increasingly detailed language to convey meaning about ideas and information. Some ways six year olds demonstrate the ability to speak easily include:

• using appropriate words to express pleasure, sadness, anger, or frustration to peers and adults in ways that make their feelings apparent;

• contributing relevant ideas to a discussion;

• offering explanations about what is happening in the classroom such as, how and why a building is being constructed in the block corner.

5

Developmental Checklists

DEVELOPMENTAL CHECKLISTS are one-page collections of performance indicators for specific grade levels. Using Checklists (one per student), teachers rate each student on each performance indicator three times during the year (fall, winter, and spring). Each indicator is rated "*Not Yet*," "*In Process*," or "*Proficient.*" On the reverse side of the Checklist is information regarding its use and detailed interpretation of its ratings system, along with space for comments.

Checklists are color coded by grade level (colors match grade-level Guidelines)

Child's identifying information

Domain names appear in white type on a black bar

Component names appear in black type on a colored bar

Indicators are listed for each component

Each indicator includes a page reference keyed to the grade-level Guidelines

Each indicator includes space to make one of three ratings ("Not Yet," "In Process," "Proficient") during the fall, winter, and spring (F, W, S)

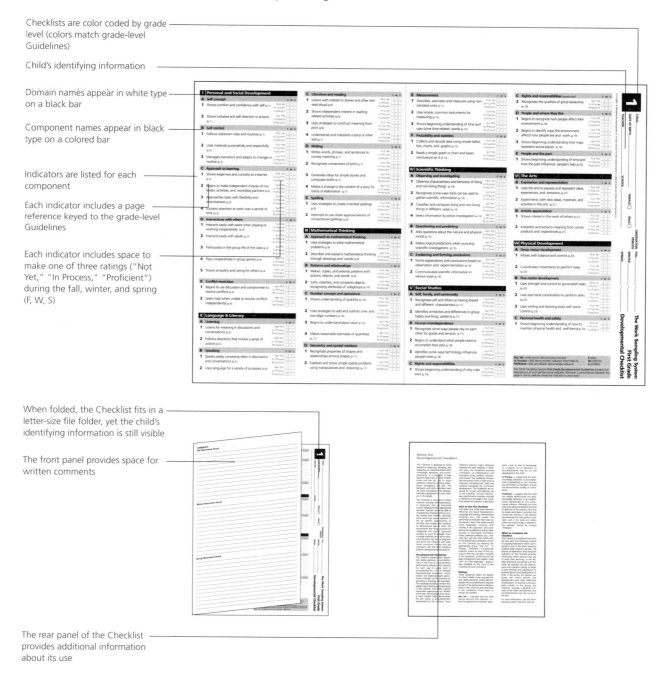

When folded, the Checklist fits in a letter-size file folder, yet the child's identifying information is still visible

The front panel provides space for written comments

The rear panel of the Checklist provides additional information about its use

Omnibus Guidelines

The OMNIBUS GUIDELINES combines six levels of the individual grade level Guidelines into a single volume organized to show continuous development. Each pair of facing pages shows the changes over time in similar indicators. There are two volumes of the Omnibus Guidelines: Vol. 1: Preschool – Third Grade, or Vol. 2: Kindergarten – Fifth Grade.

Each domain appears in the Omnibus Guidelines in its own section and begins with a brief description of the domain

Each pair of facing pages displays the performance indicators from six age or grade levels

Component name

Each indicator is followed by the rationale and examples that appear in grade-level Guidelines

Performance indicators are arranged to show continuous progress. "No equivalent performance indicator at this level" appears when a particular skill, behavior, or accomplishment does not appear in that age or grade level

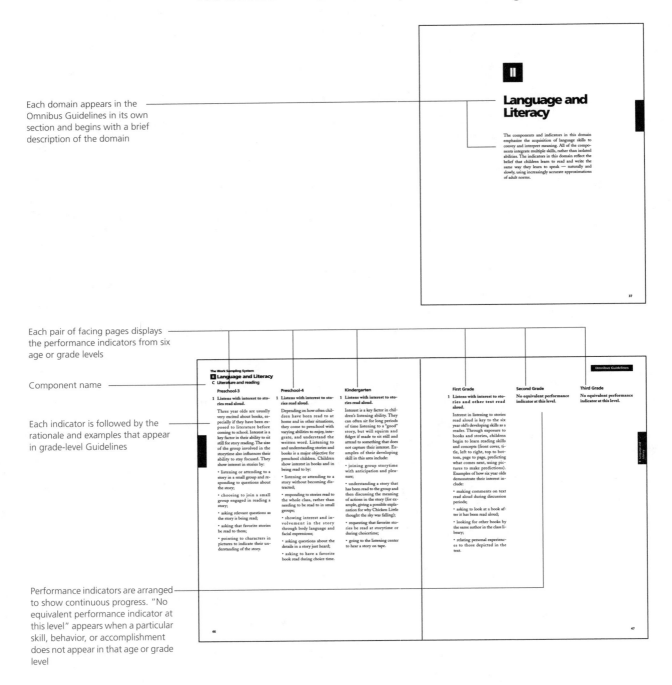

How to Use the Developmental Guidelines and Checklists

Using Guidelines and Checklists involves four steps which are listed below and described in full in the following pages.

STEP 1   Become familiar with the content of the appropriate age/grade level Developmental Guidelines (see below).

STEP 2   Set up an organizational system for gathering observational data at the beginning of the school year (see page 18).

STEP 3   Observe and document children's actions and periodically review and make preliminary ratings on the Checklist. This is a continuous process that takes place during each collection period (see page 19).

STEP 4   Make a final rating on the Checklist for each performance indicator before the end of the collection period (see page 26).

Becoming Familiar with the Guidelines

Familiarity with the contents of the Guidelines helps teachers decide what to look for as they observe, as well as describe what they can expect to see. Reading the indicators, rationales, and examples gives teachers guidance about the level of performance that can be expected from children of different ages. In this way, teacher observations and professional judgments about performance are supported by a set of explicit criteria. This helps teachers observe all children in the class with consistency and it enables teachers in different settings to observe in similar ways.

The Guidelines are *criterion-referenced.* This means that a student's work is compared to specific criteria in each domain rather than to other students' work. The Guidelines reflect decades of child development research and national, state, and local standards of curriculum development. In addition, during the initial pilot years of the Work Sampling project, teachers, curriculum specialists, and administrators from around the country contributed extensively to shaping the content of the Guidelines.

The Guidelines provide three to five *curriculum-embedded* examples of each performance indicator. The examples are intended to achieve two purposes. First, they explain and demonstrate the meaning of each indicator and help teachers understand how the indicators should be interpreted in this System. Second, they help teachers recognize the diversity of children's approaches to learning. Implicit in the Work Sampling System is the belief that children have many different ways of exhibiting their skills and knowledge.

The examples in the Guidelines are not intended to be prescriptive. Teachers should not expect to see children perform all (or even any) of

17

the examples given. Rather, the examples are intended to *illustrate* and give additional meaning to the performance indicators so that they will be interpreted similarly in different classrooms by different teachers. Children may demonstrate skills or behaviors in ways that are quite different from any of the examples offered. As long as their performance is consistent with the rationale, it is acceptable.

A preliminary reading of the Guidelines for the appropriate age/grade level provides an overview of its contents. Although the Guidelines cover a wide range of skills, knowledge, and behavior, they are by no means as comprehensive as the scope of an entire curriculum. A secondary reading should be done in which teachers review their curriculum in conjunction with the Guidelines in order to identify commonalties and differences. Teachers may wish to add items and examples that are specific to their programs but are not included in the Work Sampling System. Conversations with colleagues to discuss the relationship between specific local curricular expectations and the Work Sampling Guidelines are essential. Increased familiarity will come when teachers use the Guidelines as an ongoing reference while planning curriculum and making Checklist ratings. Teachers often find it useful to review the Guidelines one domain at a time and to consult the Omnibus Guidelines periodically to see a display of developmental expectations within that domain for children of different ages.

Creating an Organizational System for Ongoing Observation

A system for organizing observational records is essential for completing the Checklist effectively. Two possible approaches include organizing materials by student or organizing materials for the whole class by domains or time period.

Using the first approach, the teacher can establish a collection of file folders, one for each child, that can be stored in a file drawer or hanging file. Each folder contains a child's Checklist, all observation notes, notes from parents or other teachers about the child, and any other information that will contribute to making accurate Checklist ratings. An alternative is to use a loose-leaf binder divided into sections for each child. The binder can have pocket dividers to hold Checklists and pages on which Post-it notes or mailing labels can be attached. Holes can be punched in observational records such as the Work Sampling System's Process Notes (see page 20) and added to relevant sections, or notes can be written directly on loose-leaf pages.

The second approach is to keep the Checklists for all children in one folder or binder. Observational notes for all students can be organized and stored either by domain, component, or time period.

Once an organizational system is established, teachers should collect their observational records on a regular basis and periodically review and rate the Checklists.

Observing, Documenting, Reviewing, and Rating

The process of observing children, documenting their behavior, reviewing Guidelines and Checklists, and making Checklist ratings is an ongoing cycle that is repeated several times during each of the three collection periods (Figure 2). Teachers observe children continuously in the context of daily classroom activities. They document what they see using various methods of recording. Periodically, they review Checklists and make preliminary ratings based on the documentation they have collected.

FIGURE 2
Ongoing process of observing, recording, reviewing and making Checklist ratings

Observe & Record

Review & Rate

ONGOING OBSERVATION Teachers observe children in different ways throughout the day. Some of these observations are documented, either when the event occurs or after the fact. Observational notes can be made during the classroom day by stepping out of the action, or they can be made at the end of the day or week.

Since it is impossible to document everything that children do, it is a good idea to establish a routine of brief, focused observations. As part of daily or weekly planning, teachers can identify several specific opportunities that lend themselves to focused observing and recording.

Effective observation is the key to using Work Sampling Guidelines and Checklists successfully. The final section of this chapter treats the topic of observation in greater detail.

METHODS OF DOCUMENTATION The task of observing and documenting is made more manageable by having data collection techniques in place. Through trial and error, teachers can develop methods of documentation that match their personal styles. Some find it helpful to use different types of recording techniques for specific activities. The Work Sampling System provides a set of Process Note reproducible masters that teachers can use for documenting observations. As an alternative, many teachers have devised their own methods of documentation. Since it is very important to be able to record something when it is happening, materials needed for recording should be easily accessible in several places around the classroom.

Work Sampling Process Notes. The Work Sampling System provides several forms designed to facilitate the documentation process. Three reproducible masters of observational records are included in Classroom Packs and Teacher Reference Packs. Use of these forms is entirely optional. They can be reproduced or adapted to meet teachers' specific needs.

The DOMAIN PROCESS NOTES form (Figure 3) has three columns and shows all seven domains. Teachers can use this form to record observations for all developmental domains either for three children or for one child at three different times.

FIGURE 3
Domain Process Notes form

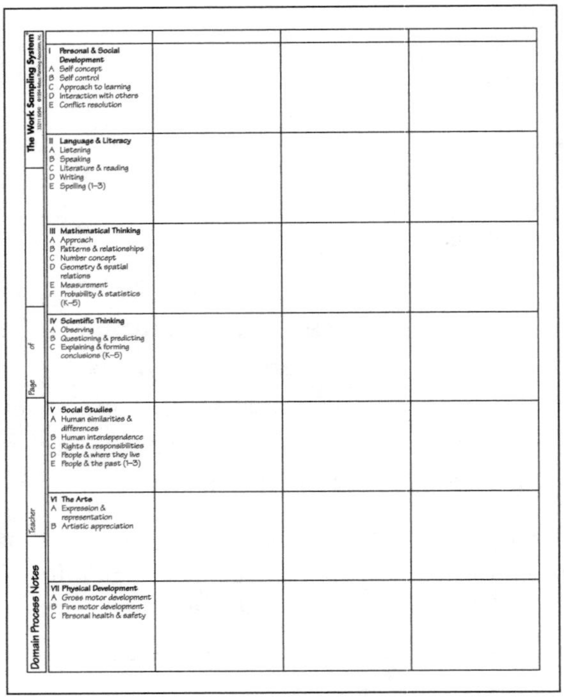
The Work Sampling System®
Domain Process Notes
Teacher
Page of

I Personal & Social Development A Self concept B Self control C Approach to learning D Interaction with others E Conflict resolution			
II Language & Literacy A Listening B Speaking C Literature & reading D Writing E Spelling (1–3)			
III Mathematical Thinking A Approach B Patterns & relationships C Number concept D Geometry & spatial relations E Measurement F Probability & statistics (K–5)			
IV Scientific Thinking A Observing B Questioning & predicting C Explaining & forming conclusions (K–5)			
V Social Studies A Human similarities & differences B Human interdependence C Rights & responsibilities D People & where they live E People & the past (1–3)			
VI The Arts A Expression & representation B Artistic appreciation			
VII Physical Development A Gross motor development B Fine motor development C Personal health & safety			

The CHILD DOMAIN PROCESS NOTES form (Figure 4) is divided into eight boxes of equal size, one for each domain and one for additional comments. It is designed to document observations for all seven domains for one child.

FIGURE 4
Child Domain Process Notes form

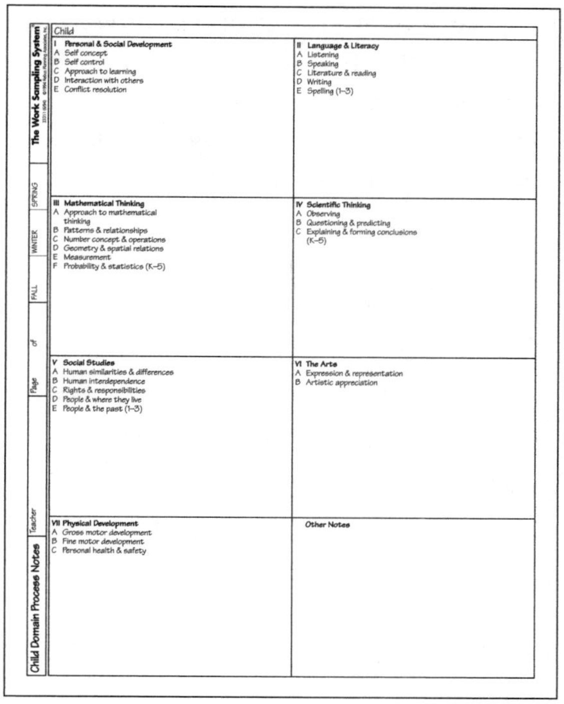

The GENERAL PROCESS NOTES form (Figure 5) consists of a 20-box grid with space to write children's names or dates of observations at the top of each box. It is open-ended and can be used in many ways, for example, to observe 20 children once, or five children at four different times, or four children during the course of a week. The boxes are the size of a small Post-it™ note (1½" x 2", 3M #653). Using Post-it notes enables teachers to transfer the notes to a child's folder easily and effectively. Some teachers write directly on the forms; after the forms are completed they are cut up and placed in the child's observation folder.

FIGURE 5
General Process Notes form

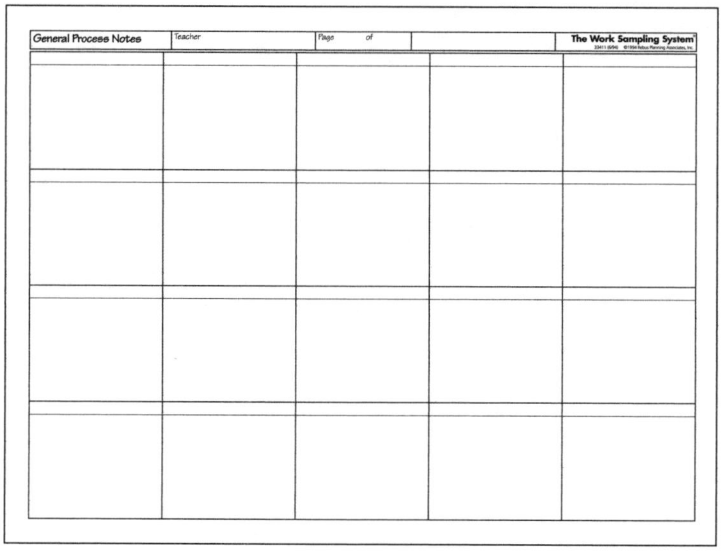

Using Work Sampling Process Notes. The figures that follow illustrate several ways that teachers have used the Work Sampling Process Notes. Figure 6 shows how one second grade teacher used the Domain Process Notes form to record her observations on two children. She used the same form for one week.

Week of 2/14	Juanita	Whitney	
I **Personal & Social Development** A Self concept B Self control C Approach to learning D Interaction with others E Conflict resolution			
III **Mathematical Thinking** A Approach B Patterns & relationships C Number concept D Geometry & spatial relations E Measurement F Probability & statistics (K–5)	2/14 wrote long story in journal — wanted to count total p. said "I can count the p. and times it by 2 to get all my sides."	2/15 3 color pattern AABCAABC w/unifix 2/16 reversals w/numbers	
IV **Scientific Thinking** A Observing B Questioning & predicting C Explaining & forming conclusions (K–5)	2/16 Observed guinea pig w/Nikki - spent time making detailed record of how g.p. eats	2/15 commented on layering of snow & ice in playgrd. Predicted it would take longer to melt than reg. snow because it was "packed so tight"	

Figure 7 shows how a third grade teacher used the Child Domain Process Notes form to document observations about Albert during a two week period.

I **Personal & Social Development** A Self concept B Self control C Approach to learning D Interaction with others E Conflict resolution	II **Language & Literacy** A Listening B Speaking C Literature & reading D Writing E Spelling (1–3)
3/9 in a fight w/Rodney about game rules for soccer — came in from recess furious — stomped around, would not sit down to talk	3/7 conf. w/him about story, he revised the ending to make it clear. He identified some spelling errors 3/18 conf. interested in Nolan Ryan-checked out book about Famous Pitchers said he knew N.R. would be in it. read 2 ch. for contract
III **Mathematical Thinking** A Approach to mathematical thinking	IV **Scientific Thinking** A Observing B Questioning & predicting

Figure 8 shows how the same third grade teacher recorded observations about her students' writing.

General Process Notes	Teacher	Page of	
Nikki	Jennifer	Albert	
3/11 Conf. to brain-storm gymnastics story. Shared her Xmas story. Good character development. Humorous "Book language" used to make transitions	3/7 Shared "The Cat, the Dog, the Bird, and Their Incredible Adventure." Works well from brainstorm. Learning to use quotation marks.	3/8 Conferenced with him about Jill or Owen story. He made revisions to make ending more clear. Also identified some spelling errors (3/7 computer)	

Other Ideas for Documentation. Many teachers have created other forms that are effective for documenting observations. Figure 9 illustrates a teacher-created form for recording the selections children make at choice time. Some other teachers have devised a technique using a legal pad (Figure 10). They cut away all the paper on the left-hand margin, leaving only the last page on which they record all the names of the children in their class. Each day they use a new sheet of paper to record observations.

Choices

Name	Mon	Tue	Wed	Thu	Fri

FIGURE 10
A teacher-created method for recording observations over time. The left margins of all pages but the last are cut away. The class list is written on the last page. Each day, a new page is used to record observations.

Other techniques that teachers use for documentation include:

- self-adhesive mailing labels

- Post-it notes

- memo pads

- index cards

As teachers observe children and document their observations, they will find a method of recording observations that works for them. There is no single way of recording that is "right." The examples given here are intended to serve as illustrations. Many other ways of collecting this information can be devised.

REVIEWING AND RATING CHECKLISTS Periodic review of the Checklists helps teachers observe the range and scope of children's development. Teachers assess what they know about a child and what they still need to find out. By reviewing and making preliminary ratings in pencil for each child two or three times during each collection period, teachers stay in touch with children's development across all domains and also identify the need for additional information. Referring to the Guidelines reminds teachers of developmentally appropriate expectations for children's performance and can spark ideas about how children demonstrate various skills, knowledge, and behaviors.

As teachers review the Checklists, they make ratings based on their observations using a three-point scale that describes performance mastery. The rating categories reflect the degree to which students have acquired the skill, knowledge, behavior, and/or demonstrated the accomplishments delineated by each performance indicator, described in the Guidelines, and listed on the Checklist. Three types of ratings are possible:

Not Yet — indicates that the skill, knowledge, or behavior has not been demonstrated

In Process — indicates that the skill, knowledge, or behavior is emergent, and is not demonstrated consistently

Proficient — indicates that the skill, knowledge, or behavior is firmly within the child's range of performance

Teachers can review Checklists in different ways. Some teachers review each child's entire Checklist. Others review one domain at a time for all the students in their class. To illustrate the process of reviewing and rating, assume a method of organization that uses one folder for each child. In this case, with information from the Guidelines in mind, the process of review would be as follows:

1 Select a child's folder.

2 Read through the observational notes.

3 Scan the Checklist. This tends to trigger memories of children's behaviors that may not have been formally documented.

4 Using pencil, make preliminary ratings of those performance indicators about which information is known. Expect to find indicators where there is not enough information to make a rating.

5 Make a notation to focus subsequent observations on the less well-known indicators. (A mark next to a performance indicator can serve as a reminder that evidence is being sought. Indicate on observational notes or in weekly plan books who and what needs be observed.)

6 Use the space for comments to write down questions, concerns, and strengths. This information will be helpful when completing the Summary Report (see Chapter 4).

It is a good idea to try to review and rate Checklists at least twice during the collection period. In this way, teachers can ensure that they have made observations about all performance indicators on the Checklist. Figure 11 illustrates an approximate time frame for reviewing and rating during a collection period.

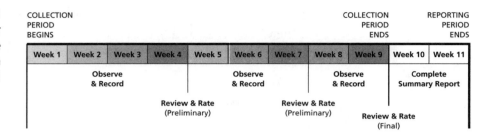

Making Final Ratings

About two weeks before the end of the reporting period, teachers make final evaluative ratings of children's performance on Checklist indicators. In order to have a basis for assessing progress over the course of the year, it is essential to "stop the clock" or halt the assessment process. Teachers may want to make their final ratings in ink.

If the Checklist covers an aspect of the curriculum that has not been included in a particular classroom, or that has not yet been introduced to a student, teachers should write "NA" for "Not Applicable." This frequently occurs at the beginning of the year.

Space is also provided on the front panel of the Checklist for brief comments. These comments elaborate on the ratings and can provide teachers with details that make their remarks in family-teacher conferences and on Summary Reports more meaningful.

Frequently Asked Questions about Guidelines and Checklists

Q *How can I find the time to observe?*

A A common misconception about observation-based assessment methods is that you have to step out of the action and watch children from a distance. Successful teachers observe children in a variety of ways, both by actively participating with them and by watching them. Both types of observation yield important information.

Observation for assessment can occur in many different ways:

- listening to students as they describe their thinking;

- talking with students as they play;

- watching how students use materials, solve problems, and interact with others;

- asking students about their work;

- listening to students as they talk with others informally, and during group discussions; and

■ reviewing student work (for example, projects, writings, drawings, reports, math problems, learning logs, journals).

Additional information about observation can be found later in this chapter (see page 33).

Q *How can I possibly observe everything that is going on in the classroom?*

A You cannot observe everything that happens in your classroom. To maximize the effectiveness of your observations, it is best that they be planned and focused. Reviewing the Guidelines in conjunction with weekly curriculum planning can help provide that focus. Devising a plan about who and what to observe as part of weekly planning makes the task of observation more systematic. Some ideas include observing:

■ one or two pupils each day;

■ a group of students for the week;

■ one domain for several days;

■ a few components of one domain during a lesson.

Becoming a skilled observer takes time and practice. Teachers usually find it beneficial to try out several observational approaches, then talk them over with colleagues and revise their plans before eventually creating a method that reflects one's personal style. Above all, it is important to try to establish a routine in which you observe and document classroom activities on a regular and consistent basis.

Q *Should I set up situations so that I can observe the skills listed on the Checklist?*

A The Work Sampling System is a curriculum-embedded assessment. Therefore, observation for Checklist ratings is intended to take place in the context of regular classroom activities. Rather than asking children to perform on-demand tasks to demonstrate their knowledge and understanding, you observe children in the context of daily classroom activities. Many times, incidental moments of the day, or children's mistakes, provide invaluable information for the Checklist.

If you have not been able to observe demonstrations of particular indicators, consider the following questions:

■ Have these children been provided with adequate opportunities and materials to practice and demonstrate these skills?

■ Is this skill or behavior one you are less familiar with, and may have more difficulty observing?

■ Have you made it possible to focus on this skill in a variety of settings?

Sometimes teachers plan a particular activity so that children can work on or practice a skill. For example, a kindergarten teacher prepares an activity with pattern blocks in order to observe the Mathematical Thinking indicator "Recognizes patterns and duplicates and extends them." Although the teacher is likely to see some children's knowledge of patterns in the context of this activity, she will probably not see it in all of the children. One child, while using pattern blocks for the first time, eagerly builds a wall of yellow hexagons instead of making a two-color pattern. It is possible that during a subsequent pattern block activity, he will construct a pattern. Another child, puts down a red block, a green block, a red block, and then a yellow, and then begins making a flower. However, during a musical chairs game, when the teacher does not expect to see patterning behavior, both children comment that the chairs are arranged in a pattern. Teachers should provide many types of activities in order to observe particular skills.

Similarly, if you do not have much expertise in science, you may only observe children during "science times" and miss their use of science concepts at other times in the day. For example, a preschool child who spontaneously puts on a hat and gloves before going outside may be showing an awareness of the weather. Similarly, the kindergartner describing bubbles at the water table or the first grader who wonders why all the pebbles in the park are the same color are both revealing some scientific understanding. Because these behaviors do not occur when you expect to see them, you may miss them.

Remember that children can express what they learn in more than one way. When you are observing for children's understanding of community workers, you may focus on children's comments during group discussion. However, some students are not active participants in class discussions. Instead, they demonstrate their knowledge of community workers during dramatic play or blocks. Often, teachers have trouble observing certain indicators because they do not consider the full range of ways that children demonstrate these skills.

When you have difficulty rating an indicator, it usually means you need further information. You may need to widen your focus and observe more broadly, in different situations, at different times of the day, and when children are interacting with different materials.

Q *How do Guidelines and Checklists help me with curriculum planning?*

A Developmental Guidelines and Checklists achieve this purpose in three different ways.

1 The Guidelines serve as a reminder to you of the breadth of the curriculum. They address seven domains and they include a wide range of activities typical of developmentally appropriate classrooms.

2 Systematic observation and documentation highlight areas of the curriculum or particular students that you may be overlooking.

3 Carefully observing children and documenting what is seen gives you an in-depth knowledge of children. This helps you plan instruction that is more responsive to individual children as well as to the class as a whole.

Because the Guidelines and Checklists emphasize continuous progress across ages and grades, you gain a sense of what your students can do now as well as where they need to go in the future. Familiarity with the Guidelines and Checklists can help teachers and students set learning goals.

Q *How can I be sure that my observations are fair?*

A To make a fair determination about whether or not a child knows or can do something, it is essential that you observe the child more than once and in more than one situation. For this reason, it is important for you to observe students repeatedly over time and to document the context of the observations.

For the assessments to be fair, students should only be evaluated on indicators that have been addressed within the context of classroom activities. It is unfair to hold children responsible for demonstrating something they have never had an opportunity to do previously or to learn. Moreover, you must bear in mind that children may have certain skills, even if they do not exhibit them in the particular contexts you have chosen. It is your responsibility to provide varied experiences within the classroom so that children can demonstrate their achievements and accomplishments.

When you use observation-based assessment, it is difficult to resist the tendency to form impressions quickly. When you have difficulty with a particular child, it is not uncommon to generalize your impressions to all encounters with that child. A child who is extremely talkative or who tends to dominate social interactions with peers may be strong in mathematics or a very talented artist; however, the child's behavior sometimes interferes with your ability to observe the child's strengths fairly. Observing as fairly as possible requires that you look at all children through the same lens. It is imperative that you train yourself to reserve judgment and to observe what the child is doing now, and how the child is approaching this task, rather than how the child may have behaved or performed in a very different situation at a different time.

Q *How can I know that my observations are valid and reliable?*

A The Work Sampling Guidelines provide a set of criteria for observation based on national and state standards and knowledge of child development. You use the Guidelines to ensure that you are observing all aspects of a child's growth and development comprehensively. Because the Guidelines describe a set of developmentally appropriate expectations, your judgments are not based simply on personal opinions but on a set of external, professional criteria. The Guidelines provide teachers with a common language and a set of shared expectations for children's learning. Teachers must interpret the Checklists and structure their observations in terms of the Guidelines. Only in this way can reliability of observations and validity of interpretations be possible.

Q *Why is it necessary to document observations?*

A Documentation forms the record or the data upon which evaluations are based. The documentation process in the Work Sampling System has two steps. The first step is the informal note-taking that you do on a regular basis. The second consists of the ratings you make on the Work Sampling Checklist that are supported by your informal observational notes. Documenting observations is important for four reasons.

1 Written records help you keep track of what children know and can do. They remind you of a child's strengths and weaknesses.

2 Written records collected over time enable you to see patterns in behaviors and approaches to learning.

3 You can use your written observations of children to plan instructional activities that are more responsive to children's interests and needs.

4 Recorded observations provide evidence to support your judgments in the assessment process.

Without careful documentation, the reliability of checklist ratings decreases and the validity of your judgments is compromised.

Q *Are Checklists sent home?*

A Checklists are not designed to be sent home. They are written in language for teachers. However, parents always have access to the Checklist should they request it, and you may wish to use the Checklists during conferences to help families understand how their child is doing in a particular domain.

Q *Is it possible for a rating to change from "Proficient" to "In Process" from the fall to the spring?*

A Although the Guidelines describe developmental expectations for performance indicators in broad terms, you complete Checklists based on your expectations for a particular time of year. For example, when evaluating a child's performance for the Checklist in November, you consider what you have taught and your expectations of children at that time, and then make your ratings accordingly. A child who was using several reading strategies in the fall of second grade to read simple books might be rated "Proficient" on the Checklist because that was the fall expectation. However, by spring, the expectation is that children will be reading more difficult material. If the child is still reading only simple books, his rating at this time will be "In Process."

Q *Can I use the Checklist during parent-teacher conferences?*

A Although reviewing the entire Checklist during a conference would take too much time, some teachers find it helpful to refer to particular sections of the Checklist as a way to offer specific information about a child's strengths or weaknesses or to illustrate a rating on the Summary Report. In some instances, using the Checklist with parents may not be appropriate. Checklists are written in professional language. The amount and organization of information recorded on the Checklist is complex and may be overwhelming to a parent in the context of a brief conference.

Q *How can specialists be involved in completing Checklists?*

A Specialists can contribute a great deal to the richness and detail of the Checklist. The more information you have about students, the more accurate your assessment. Collaboration and dialogue among all of the adults who work with children will enhance accuracy. The Guidelines should be shared with special subject and resource teachers so that they can channel appropriate information to you. These teachers can give the child's primary teacher either anecdotal notes or data relevant to their subject areas, all of which can be used to inform the Work Sampling Checklist. Having conferences with special subject teachers can be a useful way to gather this information. An optional Special Subject Report form (see page 107) has been devised and is available for use by specialists. (For further discussion of these issues, see page 121.)

Q *Why are Checklists filled out three times during the school year?*

A Children grow and change at different rates between ages 3 and 11. Their growth often occurs quite rapidly. As children change, you form new images of their abilities based on their current performance, and you may forget some of the details of their prior abilities. Only by noting a child's specific performance at one time point can you later truly assess the child's progress. For this reason, the Work Sampling System advocates a three-times-per-year framework for assessment. This way the child's profile of skills and knowledge in one collection period can be compared with his/her profile in an earlier period. This facilitates assessment of progress and provides a chance to record change in performance.

Q *What happens to the Checklist at the end of the year?*

A At the end of the year, you may decide to include the Checklist in the child's school file so that it can be reviewed by the child's next teacher. At the beginning of the next year, the new teacher has the opportunity to scan the spring ratings on the Checklists and obtain a starting point for review and instruction. This can be particularly helpful since the Work Sampling System is continuous from one grade to the next.

Although parents have legal access to all information about their children, the Checklists are not intended to be sent home at the end of the year because they have been written with educators, rather than parents, in mind.

Q *How long does it take to learn how to use the Guidelines and Checklists?*

A After the first two collection periods, most teachers have internalized much of the information included in the Guidelines for the grade levels they teach. Although they may occasionally refer back to the Guidelines, they do it much less frequently than earlier in the school year.

The greatest difficulty teachers have in completing the Checklists is integrating the observing, documenting, reviewing, and rating cycle into their daily schedules. This process is facilitated by:

- Observing and recording selectively, instead of trying to document everything all the time.

- Planning when, how, and what will be observed each week.

- Finding strategies that feel comfortable for documenting.

Q *How long does it take to complete the Checklist?*

A The answer to this question depends on individual work style. If you review and rate the Checklist in an ongoing way, scanning the Checklist takes less than five minutes, and reviewing all the information collected in order to make final ratings will take about 15 minutes per child. If rating particular indicators is very difficult or time consuming, you probably need more information about the child, and should continue to observe.

Q *Which Checklist should I use for children above or below grade-level expectations?*

A Development in children is rarely even. Many children who function above or below grade-level do not do so in all domains. Rather, they may be at grade-level for some domains while being above or below expectations in others. For example, a child who is very mature verbally may be less so socially. Because of this natural variability, we recommend that you use as a starting point the Checklist that corresponds to the child's chronological age.

For those children who are functioning very differently from expectations, information from the Omnibus Guidelines can be used to increase your understanding of the areas in which the child is above or below grade-level. The examples in the Guidelines help you to modify your instructional plans to reflect the child's skills and knowledge in all of the domains. The Summary Report should also be used to address the areas in which the child is performing above or below grade-level. Particularly for the child who is working below grade-level, it is important to describe what the child is doing and accomplishing well, not only what the child's areas of difficulty are.

Q *How are the Guidelines and Checklists used in multi-age classrooms?*

A Work Sampling fits well with multi-age classrooms because of the emphasis in these classrooms on the continuum of children's development. By examining all six levels of an indicator presented in the Omnibus, teachers can gain an understanding of what comes before and what comes after each grade-level indicator. However, although the Omnibus presents several levels of development at once, the Checklists do not.

Teachers of multi-age groups use several different Checklists to cover the ages represented by their students. Thus, if you have a class of 7 and 8 year olds, use both the second grade and the third grade Checklists. Because all of the domains, most of the components, and many of the indicators are the same across grade levels, you need not learn entirely new information for each grade represented in your classroom, although the rationales and examples are usually different at different grade levels. The Omnibus Guidelines enable you to find these similarities and differences, and to move easily between grade levels so that you can find the right place for each child.

Further Discussion about Guidelines and Checklists

Observation

Observation in the Work Sampling System occurs in the context of the ongoing classroom routine. Assessing children in the context of the regular classroom provides a representative picture of skills, knowledge, and behaviors. Because evaluation is not based on a narrow sample of these skills, but on many observations, teachers have repeated opportunities to evaluate the child's skills, knowledge, and behaviors.

Children tell us a great deal through their actions and language. Careful observation over time can reveal important information about children's individual strengths and difficulties. By observing children, teachers are exposed not only to what children know but to how they know it — their process of thinking and learning. Observation helps teachers find answers to questions that include:

- How does the child approach tasks?

- How does the child use language to express thinking?

- How does the child use materials?

- How does the child engage in social tasks with others?

Because children demonstrate skills differently depending on the context, it is essential to observe children in a wide range of classroom activities and at different times of the day. Teachers can use what they learn from observation to guide children's learning.

TEACHERS AS OBSERVERS Teachers observe in three different ways:

1 by participating in the action;

2 by stepping out of the action for short periods of time;

3 by reflecting on the action after it has occurred.

Each of these approaches makes it possible to collect the evidence necessary for documenting children's learning on the Developmental Checklist. Each will be discussed in turn.

Participating in the action. Teachers are typically in the midst of classroom action. They may be conferring with one student, teaching a lesson to a small group, or having a discussion with the entire class. They watch what children are doing, listen to what they are saying, note who they are working with, and ask questions to find out more about children's thinking. Observing in this way provides teachers with a wealth of information, which is often difficult to remember because so much is taking place simultaneously.

It is essential to establish realistic expectations about how much is possible to record in these settings. When working with one student, more can be documented than when leading a group. Figure 12 shows how a teacher created a form for each child's reading inventory which she uses to document her individual reading conferences with children. The various types of Work Sampling Process Notes can also be useful when working with a single child (see pages 20 – 23).

FIGURE 12
Teacher-created reading inventory allows the teacher to record choices and to make quick comments

Reading Inventory		
Name _____		
Book Title	Date	Comments

When working with a group of children, the task of recording meaning-ful observations is more difficult. Sentence-length comments and anec-dotal records are nearly impossible to record. Some teachers have cre-ated a type of shorthand code made up of checkmarks and other symbols recorded on a class list grid (Figure 13). For this approach to work, the teacher must anticipate the types of expected observations and write them in the header above each column on the grid. The coding used can be simple, with just a few symbols, or quite complex, with a wide variety of symbols, multiple marks in the same grid square to record multiple occurrences of behavior, and even one- or two-word comments.

FIGURE 13
A teacher-created class list form. Using checkmarks and other symbols, teachers can document observations for an entire class while participating in the action.

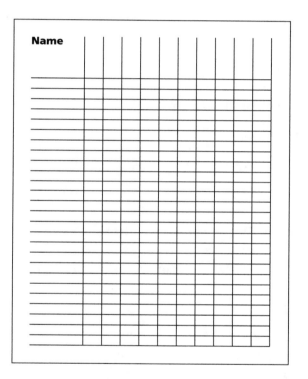

Whether working with a single child or a group, planning and focusing are important keys to successful documentation. Teachers should not expect to record meaningfully every possible behavior. An enormous amount of information can be obtained while participating in the action, but it will often lack the detail and richness possible when making longer and more reflective comments.

Stepping out of the action. Stepping out of the action to observe is an extremely effective way to learn about children. It allows the teacher to focus on one child at a time. She may watch how the child interacts with others or how the child approaches a learning task. When teachers are in the midst of classroom action, they do many things simultaneously, such as motivating children, communicating information, keeping chil-dren engaged, providing materials, and teaching skills. Stepping out of the action enables teachers to suspend these tasks for a few moments and to be completely receptive to what is happening around them.

Stepping out of the action to observe does not require large amounts of time. Teachers who take three to five minutes a day to step back and observe one or two children can collect a great deal of important information. Rather than being overly ambitious and setting aside large amounts of time, it is much more effective to develop the habit of observing for just a few minutes several times each day. Example 1 shows anecdotal notes taken in this way by a preschool teacher:

EXAMPLE 1

4/6 Recci: Dramatic Play
As I approach the house area, Recci is playing with the doctor's kit. He silently administers oxygen to a doll, takes its temperature, and tests its reflexes. He uses the stethoscope and says, "I can hear his heart for real." He uses the blood pressure cuff, asking for help from Lisa in attaching it to the doll's arm.

Iola enters the house area, and asks Lisa who is also playing in the house, "Who are you being?" She replies, "Doctor." Iola then asks Recci. He says, "A nurse." Iola asks, "What can I be?" Recci says, "You're the mom." He hands her the doll and gives the doll a shot. He says, "Ouch!"

Reflecting on the action after the fact. Reflecting after the fact suggests two different types of teacher actions. The first involves taking a moment after an event occurs or at the end of the day to document what transpired. The second entails reviewing children's work as a way to reflect on their learning.

Teachers make mental notes in the midst of classroom action all the time. By taking a few minutes during a break in the day (for example, during rest time, quiet reading, or journal time) or at the end of a day or week, teachers can record some notes about events that occurred. They can recall a math period and some of the strategies they observed children using, or a discussion and some comments children made. It is both unnecessary and unrealistic to think about recording something about every child or every event in the day. However, when teachers get in the habit of making a few notes about one or two children or events each day or every few days, these records add up to substantial documentation of what children know and can do.

When teachers review children's work at the end of the day or week, their notes about children's learning inform the Checklist. What does the work show? What skills and knowledge are expressed in the work? Does the work reflect the assignment? Looking at children's work also reminds teachers of the context in which the work was created. What was the child doing? What was the activity? How did the child approach the task? Did the child show interest in the task? What else was going on in the classroom at that time? Reviewing a domain of the Guidelines or Checklist prior to looking at children's work can help to focus this reflection. Example 2 illustrates how a preschool teacher reflected on the action after the fact.

EXAMPLE 2   *Nkrumah is currently working on controlling the mouse on the computer. He understands that he needs to put the cursor arrow on an object to activate it, but has difficulty coordinating movements to do so. When using the keyboard, he tends to press the screen occasionally instead of pressing a key.*

WHAT TO WRITE   Writing things down ensures that they will be remembered. The process of informal note-taking and record keeping provides teachers with the evidence they need to make informed evaluative decisions about ratings for the Checklist. Anecdotal records are brief narrative descriptions of a child's actions. They are records of the facts of an event which might include what the child did, what the child said, what materials the child used, when the event occurred, and with whom the child worked. Anecdotes can be long or short and can describe an event that was observed from a distance or one in which the teacher was a participant.

Recording action or opinion. Documenting observations effectively requires that teachers differentiate between what they actually see and hear and their own opinions and interpretations of these actions. When observing children at work and play, language that describes their actions is more informative than words that convey judgment. For example, Jeremy, a first grader, is working with Cuisenaire rods to solve a series of math problems. Examples 3 and 4 show how two teachers might have documented his work.

EXAMPLE 3   *11/4: 10 a.m. — Jeremy is scattered and too distracted to do his work.*

EXAMPLE 4   *11/4: 10 a.m. — Jeremy has worked on math for 15 min — completed one problem of five. Builds with rods. Talks continually w/ others about baseball. Walked to and from pencil sharpener and water fountain many times.*

Although both records convey that Jeremy is not actually completing his math work, the first gives only the teacher's impressions. The second record describes Jeremy's actions and provides enough detailed information to explain why he is not completing his work. It allows the teacher to ask questions about how to support Jeremy's success as a learner: Is Jeremy distracted? Is he more interested in baseball? Would it help to engage Jeremy's interest by relating the math problems to baseball? Would he be more successful if he could work collaboratively on the problems with others? Questions and interpretations/impressions can be included in the documentation of an observation, but should be clearly identified as such. As illustrated in Example 5, some teachers divide their records into two parts. On one side they write observations. On the other side they note questions, concerns, and interpretations of behavior.

EXAMPLE 5

Notes	Interpretations
11/4: 10 a.m. *Jeremy has worked on math for 15 min —* *completed one problem of five. Builds with* *rods. Talks continually w/ others about* *baseball. Walked to and from pencil* *sharpener and water fountain many times.*	*Distracted?* *Why?*

HOW MUCH TO WRITE Deciding how much to write depends on two factors: what you are trying to learn, and what the circumstances of the observation are. Different methods of recording make different demands on teachers' time and energy, as well as providing the teacher with different kinds of information. For example, using brief notes, the teacher can document the occurrence and frequency of children's behaviors. With anecdotal records, the teacher can describe particular events that occur during the day, the process a child used in working on a project, or an interaction between two students.

Learning about how a child thinks, solves problems, uses materials, and interacts with others demands highly descriptive records. Describing *how* a child does something is more informative than simply stating *that* a child did something. Recording that a child spoke during a group activity is less informative than keeping track of what the child said, as Example 6 illustrates.

EXAMPLE 6

2/17 Dwight
When cooking cranberry sauce with the class, Dwight said, "I can see a lot of steam," as the sugar and water were heating. When the cranberries were added, he noted that, "I see bubbles coming up there." He commented that the finished product, "... looks like juice."

In these examples, by recording specific dialogue, the teacher learns more about children's understanding of concepts.

How much is recorded depends on the amount of time a teacher has and the types of activities in which children engage. When working with one child in a reading or writing conference, it may be possible to write a great deal. During a group lesson or discussion, quick check marks on a class list may be all that is feasible.

Focused observation informs instructional planning. Deciding to observe and document children's learning regularly and in the context of ongoing classroom activities can lead to more effective teaching. Watching and listening to children closely and with an open mind enables teachers to recognize the diverse ways children demonstrate what they know and can do. Consistent observation, documentation, and review of Guidelines and Checklists can inform instructional planning in several ways.

The relationship between curriculum and assessment lies in using an approach to assessment that allows teachers both to learn about their students and to plan learning opportunities that are responsive to students' achievements and interests. Teachers get to know children well by observing them consistently and systematically. Because the Guidelines provide teachers with a set of clear developmental expectations, teachers can plan curricula that allow children to be challenged and successful.

Many teachers find it helpful to review the Guidelines and Checklists as they plan their weekly curriculum. In this way, they can structure activities with the goal of being able to observe particular performance indicators. Used in this way, the Guidelines and Checklists can also serve as a reminder about all curriculum domains. The examples in the Guidelines are intended to encourage teachers' thinking about the broad range of opportunities they can offer children. This is especially valuable as teachers plan those areas of the curriculum about which they feel less confident.

When teachers review Checklists to make initial ratings at the midpoint of a collection period, they often discover that there is something about a particular child that they knew very little about. Teachers can then plan curriculum experiences designed to learn more about that aspect of the child. Some children have particularly dominant characteristics: they are very verbal in group discussions; they are good at math; they are disruptive in meetings; they are quiet; or they are excellent artists. When a child has a dominant characteristic, it is common for teachers to view the entire child in that way. Studying the child's Checklist can be a way to expand a teacher's thinking about other aspects of the child's growth and learning.

Using the Guidelines for Professional Development

The Guidelines can form the basis of professional development and dialogue for teachers about assessment. Teachers can work together to generate additional age-appropriate examples for the Guidelines. Of particular value to teachers has been generating examples that reflect diverse learning styles and cultural backgrounds.

In addition, teachers work with colleagues to review the Guidelines in conjunction with their school or district curriculum. In doing so, teachers may decide to elaborate indicators that directly reflect their curriculum goals. Because the Guidelines describe expectations for the entire year, some teachers find it helpful to discuss their expectations for each collection period.

Finally, teachers use the Guidelines as a basis for discussion about the types of learning experiences they provide for children. Talking with grade-level colleagues enables teaches to reflect on their practice. Some questions to consider include:

- Are children having adequate opportunities to reveal their skills and knowledge?

- Are the same children always being noticed?

- Have science, social studies, and art experiences been offered?

- What types of experiences would help less verbal children demonstrate what they know?

Involving Students in the Assessment Process

Although children's involvement in the process of observation and Checklist completion is indirect, it is very important. Observation of children should not be kept hidden from them. When teachers let children know that they are observing and when they share their observations, children can become more active role in being responsible and independent learners. Children can be involved in the Checklist assessment process in two ways. First, the teacher should make explicit to children what they are learning and why they are learning it. Second, the teacher should discuss with children what is being assessed and how this process occurs. Placing in a prominent location the Wall Chart of performance indicators that comes with the grade-level Guidelines, and discussing it with the class is a way to begin this process.

Adults rarely make the reasons for learning skills and knowledge explicit to children. Teachers can use class discussions and informal conversations with children to help them consider why they are learning particular skills and knowledge. A teacher might say, "Let's think about why we need to use legible handwriting. Who can think of some reasons?" Or, "Why does it make sense to know more than one way for adding and subtracting numbers?" When teachers encourage children to be reflective about why they need to learn particular skills, they are likely to increase students' motivation to learn.

It is extremely important for children to know what and when teachers are evaluating. When children are writing in a journal and are concentrating on expressing their feelings, they may not be focusing on spelling or handwriting. However, if teachers intend to assess spelling and handwriting as well as the expression of feelings, children should be informed of this. Too often, the criteria teachers use for evaluation are not made explicit to children. Therefore, children do not have the chance to make the specific type of effort needed in order to be successful. It is not enough to assume or expect that children will always do their best work. Teachers should be specific about which expectations apply in particular situations.

It is extremely valuable for teachers to have discussions with students about how teachers find out what children know. For example, a teacher might pose the question, "Why do you think I take notes during a reading conference?" or "Why do you think I write down some of what you say during meeting time?" When children are made aware of the teacher's role as observer and recorder, they are more likely to understand why there are times when the teacher is not available to them.

Conclusion

A major part of the teacher's job is to observe students during the course of each school day and to use these observations for educational decision-making. The ongoing activities of observing, documenting, reviewing, and rating help teachers stay alert to each child's development. As teachers gain familiarity with the Guidelines and develop methods and routines suited to their personal styles, documentation tasks that at first seemed time consuming become integrated into the school day.

The Work Sampling System's Developmental Guidelines provide structure and organization for teachers' observations by identifying children's age-related behaviors, knowledge, and skills. The Checklists help keep track of children's accomplishments by providing teachers with a method for summarizing and recording their observations during the school year.

Together, the Developmental Guidelines and Checklists help teachers place children's development within a framework of reasonable expectations and provide a means for evaluating student achievement accurately, consistently, and meaningfully. The Guidelines and Checklists serve as profiles of children's growth across curriculum domains, profiles that are then elaborated by the more specific information collected in the Portfolio and summarized on the Summary Report.

CHAPTER 3

Portfolios

Collecting, Selecting, and Evaluating Student Work

THIS CHAPTER ADDRESSES THE SECOND ELEMENT OF THE WORK SAMpling System — Portfolio Collection. The chapter is divided into five sections:

- Introduction to the Portfolio Collection Process

- The Structure and Organization of the Work Sampling Portfolio

- The Process of Portfolio Collection

- Frequently Asked Questions about the Portfolio Collection Process

- Further Discussion about Portfolios

Introduction to the Portfolio Collection Process

Throughout the course of each school day, students' learning activities result in the creation of products ranging from journal entries to collages, from plans for scientific investigations to block constructions, from solutions of math problems to poems. Many products or examples of student work can be collected in a Work Sampling System Portfolio. Some types of work (for example, block structures) cannot be put in a Portfolio, although a representation of the work can be included, such as a photograph, or a pencil drawing with accompanying text that explains the process and results of the construction. Work samples collected in a Portfolio document the child's knowledge, skills, accomplishments, and approach to learning.

As students engage in classroom activities, teachers and students can review, discuss, and evaluate the resulting work. Teachers can help children understand why the work is important, what features of the work are significant, and whether the work shows progress. Together, teachers and students can select examples of work to be included in the Portfolio. As children grow and develop, they can take increasing responsibility for independently reviewing and evaluating their work. In selecting Portfolio items and reflecting upon them, children begin to develop personal standards for evaluating their own work.

The Work Sampling Portfolio is intended to create a portrait of the child as a learner — and to tell a story about the child's learning over time. Unlike the Developmental Checklists that specifically document the broad scope of a child's learning, the Portfolio provides an in-depth portrait that shows the unique characteristics of an individual child's work and the kinds of learning activities that have occurred in the child's classroom. In this way, the Portfolio is another important source of information for the evaluations recorded on the Summary Report.

Description

Portfolios are purposeful collections of children's work that illustrate the quality of children's work, their progress, and achievements. The Work Sampling System Portfolio contains two kinds of items — Core Items and Individualized Items — that are collected on three occasions during the course of the year.

Purpose

The Portfolio serves several important purposes, including:

1   Showing the *quality* of children's work and thinking across the curriculum;

2   Demonstrating children's *progress* and growth over time;

3   *Involving children* in assessing their own work; and

4   Assisting teachers with *instructional planning*.

Features of the Work Sampling Portfolio

Saving children's work is an activity that is familiar to most teachers. What is new about the Work Sampling Portfolio is the structured framework it provides to help teachers make decisions about which examples of work to save.

■   The Work Sampling Portfolio is organized by the collection of two types of work: Core Items and Individualized Items.

■   Work is collected during three collection periods: fall, winter, and spring.

■   Students and teachers jointly make decisions about work to be included in the Portfolio.

■ Work Sampling Classroom Packs and Student Materials Packs include the following materials designed to facilitate portfolio collection:

- Portfolio Item Record Post-it™ notes;

- Core Item Collection Plan reproducible master;

- Thoughts About My Portfolio form reproducible master; and

- Portfolio domain labels.

Structure and Organization of the Work Sampling Portfolio

The structure of the Work Sampling Portfolio is determined by the collection of Core Items and Individualized Items. This structure helps create a portrait of the whole child without overloading the Portfolio with too many items.

File folder (or other container) for Individualized items

Five file folders (or other containers) for Core Items in five of the seven Work Sampling domains

Core Item Collection Plan summarizes contents of Core Item folders

Accordion file (or other container)

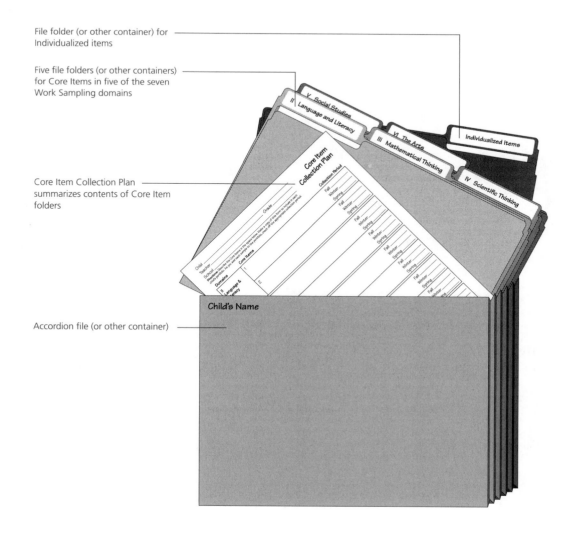

Core Items

DEFINITION Core Items are representations of particular areas of learning within each of five domains. Their purpose is to show the quality and progress of children's domain-related learning.

EXPLANATION OF CORE ITEM COLLECTION Two Core Items are collected from each of five domains three times during the year from all children in a classroom. Core Items are designed to ensure that work is collected from multiple domains in order to represent the breadth of the child's development. Because each domain encompasses many areas of learning, a single sample of work from any of these areas does not accurately represent the child's work in the entire domain. For this reason, two Core Items per domain are collected in order to represent the breadth of learning within a domain. Nevertheless, it is not expected that the two Core Items will provide a comprehensive portrait of the child's work in each domain, only a representative sample of his/her performance in that domain.

1   Teachers and students collect Core Items from five of the seven Work Sampling domains. These domains are:

- Language and Literacy
- Mathematical Thinking
- Scientific Thinking
- Social Studies
- The Arts

These domains lend themselves to concrete representations of student work and thinking. In preschools Core Items may be collected from Personal and Social Development and from Physical Development. However, because work in these two domains usually does not result in a product or other type of representation that can easily be saved in a Portfolio, Core Items from these domains are not generally included as part of the Work Sampling Portfolio.

2   Core Items are collected in the fall, winter, and spring. Comparing later work with earlier work that documents the same area of learning allows teachers and students to observe and evaluate progress.

3   Core Items are collected from all children in a class. Although representations of the same area of learning will be collected from each child, the examples of work selected are likely to be unique to each child. By collecting Core Items from all of their students, teachers see many different examples of work in each area of learning. This enhances teachers' understanding of how to set standards for work in their classroom.

Individualized Items

DEFINITION Individualized items are samples of children's work that capture their unique characteristics and reflect the integration of curriculum domains. Unlike Core Items, they are not planned in advance by the teacher, nor tied to specific domains. Instead, they represent a child's interests, approaches to learning, and significant accomplishments, and may reflect learning from several curricular domains simultaneously.

EXPLANATION OF INDIVIDUALIZED ITEM COLLECTION A minimum of five Individualized Items are selected for the Portfolio at the end of each collection period. The kind of work selected as Individualized Items can vary from one collection period to another and will likely be different for each child.

Total Number of Portfolio Items

By the end of the school year, each child's Portfolio will contain 45 items:

	5	domains	
x	2	Core Items per domain	(per collection period)
=	**10**	**Core Items**	(per collection period)
+	5	Individualized Items	(per collection period)
=	**15**	**Items per collection period**	
x	3	Collection periods per year	
=	**45**	**Items per year**	

The Process of Portfolio Collection

The Work Sampling System Portfolio collection process can be divided into the four stages listed here and described in the following pages:

1 Planning and preparation (see page 48)

2 Collection (see page 54)

3 Selection (see page 59)

4 Evaluation (see page 64)

Except for planning, each of the other three stages occurs in an ongoing manner during each collection period, and each is enhanced by notes or documentation by the teacher or student.

Portfolios are created so that they can be studied by different audiences. Although the child, the classroom teacher, and the child's family comprise the primary audience, other viewers might include another teacher, a specialist interested in the child's development, or an administrator. For some audiences, work samples may only be meaningful when accompanied by explanations. In fact, explanations or documentation attached to the actual work sample are sometimes as important as the sample of work itself. The explanation may include a description of what the work is, how it was created, and why it is included. Because teachers cannot provide detailed comments and descriptions for each piece of work, they must decide what information will be most informative when the work is evaluated. Discussion of how to document work samples appears throughout this section of the Portfolio collection process.

Planning and Preparation

The first stage of the Portfolio collection process has four steps:

STEP 1   Create individual Portfolios.

STEP 2   Decide how and where to store Portfolios.

STEP 3   Prepare work folders.

STEP 4   Plan Core Items.

CREATING INDIVIDUAL PORTFOLIOS Although teachers use various methods for organizing individual portfolios, two approaches are most common. The first is to use six file folders placed inside an accordion file for each student. Five of the folders contain work in the five domains represented by Core Items (Language and Literacy, Mathematical Thinking, Scientific Thinking, Social Studies, The Arts). A sixth folder holds Individualized Items (Figure 1).

FIGURE 1
Individual Portfolio using accordion file and file folders

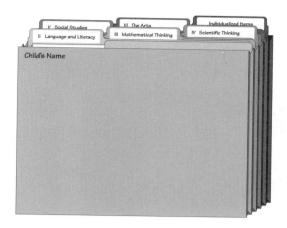

Figure 2 illustrates a second commonly used approach. Teachers use four pocket folders held together with a spiral binding. One of the pockets stores the Core Item Collection Plan, five pockets represent Core Item domains, and the remaining pockets store Individualized Items.

FIGURE 2
Individual Portfolio using pocket folders with spiral binding

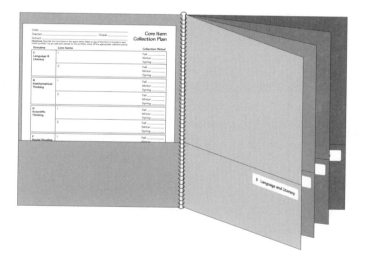

Using either method, teachers store Core Items together by domain, in chronological order, to facilitate the evaluation of progress. Individualized Items are organized within their folder by collection period. Teachers can use the pre-printed domain labels that are available in the Work Sampling System Classroom Pack.

Other methods for Portfolio construction include ring binders, large construction paper folded in half and stapled, hanging files, covered plastic tubs, and boxes. When teachers introduce Portfolios to children, they often invite students to decorate their Portfolios.

DECIDING HOW AND WHERE TO STORE PORTFOLIOS Once Portfolios have been created for each child in the classroom, teachers decide how and where to store them. Milk crates (Figure 3), file cabinets or drawers, shelves, plastic or rubber tubs, and boxes can be used to store Portfolios. Some preschool teachers have made wall hangings with pockets for each child's Portfolio (Figure 4).

FIGURE 3 (LEFT)
A milk crate used to store Portfolios

FIGURE 4 (RIGHT)
A preschool teacher created a wall hanging with pockets to store Portfolios

If Portfolio collection is to become an integral part of the classroom, it is essential that Portfolios be stored in a location that is both visible and accessible to children. Some teachers divide the class Portfolios and store them in two or more different locations around the room. In this way, children are less likely to crowd into a single location in the classroom when it is time to work with their Portfolios.

PREPARING WORK FOLDERS Many teachers create a place for children's work to be collected in an ongoing way before being placed in the Portfolio. Student work can be filed in "work folders" that may consist of separate sets of file folders, mailboxes, cubbies, sets of drawers, shelves, or other containers.

Some teachers collect all samples of children's work in the folder and review it periodically. Others establish a folder called "Possible Portfolio Samples" in which teachers and children place work that may eventually be included in the portfolio.

PLANNING CORE ITEMS Core Items originate in teacher planning. The first step in developing Core Items is to choose two areas of learning within each of the five Core Item domains. The areas should reflect two curriculum strands within the domain that will remain important throughout the year.

Choosing areas of learning. To select areas of learning, teachers identify a domain and begin to list important goals for students within that domain. When selecting areas of learning, they should consider the following:

■ Areas of learning should be concepts or processes, rather than specific content (such as themes, units, and chapters).

■ Areas of learning should be something that children are learning throughout the school year and that warrant year-long attention.

■ Areas of learning should be defined precisely enough so that different examples of work can be compared in order to show growth over time.

Based on their curricula, teachers identify two broad areas of learning central to their goals for students. Language and Literacy, for example, is a large domain that comprises multiple curriculum emphases (such as writing, reading, and speaking). A teacher may select writing and reading comprehension as areas of learning. This decision implies that children will be engaged in this kind of learning frequently and will create many products that reflect this learning throughout the year.

After selecting an area of learning, the next step in planning Core Items is to review curriculum activities that the teacher uses to engage children in the selected area of learning. Teachers may use a Core Item planning worksheet (Figure 5) to help keep track of the types of experiences they already offer children within the designated area of learning. After teachers identify the domain and area of learning within that domain, they list the curriculum activities that engage children in the learning area selected. For each activity, the teacher lists different types of work that may result from the activity or that may represent the learning. Examples 1 and 2 show two completed Core Item planning worksheets.

FIGURE 5
Core Item planning worksheet

Core Item Planning Worksheet

Domain:

A record or representation of:

Classroom Activities	Child's Work

EXAMPLE 1   **Core Item Planning Worksheet**

Domain: *Scientific Thinking*

A record or representation of: *how the child accurately observes and records scientific phenomena*

Classroom activities	Child's work
Observing the life cycles of butterflies	*Drawings with or without captions*
Observing and recording items in a collection (e.g., shells, rocks, seeds, feathers)	*Drawings, paintings, dictations, or photographs of plasticene models*
Observing animal behaviors	*Videotape of dramatization, drawings or paintings with dictations*
Construction of bridges with blocks, straws, or other materials after observing them first hand	*Photographs of structures with descriptions*
Experimentation with properties of magnets	*Drawn or written descriptions of observations*
Observing behaviors of earth worms	*Anecdotal record of the child's observation, play dough models, dictated descriptions*
Observing classroom pets	*Drawing and written or dictated descriptions*
Observation of plant growth	*Easel paintings, drawings, dictated or written descriptions*

EXAMPLE 2   **Core Item Planning Worksheet**

Domain: *Mathematical Thinking*

A record or representation of: *the child's understanding of increasingly complex patterns*

Classroom activities	Child's work
Creating block patterns	*Drawings, photographs and written or dictated descriptions*
Working with unifix cubes, beads, pegboards, or other manipulative materials	*Tracings, cut-out pictures, drawings, photographs, each with descriptions (written or dictated)*
Block building	*Photograph with description*
Drawing and painting	*Drawings, paintings, written or dictated descriptions*
Weaving	*Weavings with written or dictated descriptions*
Rhythm activities or clapping games	*Video or audio tape, or anecdotal description*

After completing the worksheet, it should become clear that a single area of learning can be represented in many ways. In fact, Core Items are designed to accommodate different approaches to learning and different ways that children represent their learning. Although the Core Item represents the same area of learning for all students in the classroom throughout the year, the actual work samples included in each child's Portfolio will be different. Figures 6 and 7 illustrate two ways that kindergarten children in the same classroom demonstrated their knowledge of patterns.

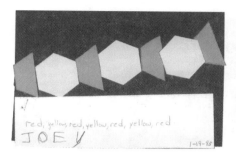

The focus on an area of learning, rather than a specific type of work, provides flexibility in the selection of the Core Items for the Portfolio. A child need not be limited to approaching this learning in the same way throughout the year. For example, in the domain of Mathematical Thinking, an area of learning might be the understanding of *sorting* and *classifying*. One child's Portfolio may have a collage of food pictures pasted into their respective food groups in the fall, a drawing representing classification of pattern blocks by shape and color in the winter, and some writing describing the rule used to classify animals in the spring. Figures 8 and 9 show different fall and spring representations of patterning by a third grader. Examples of possible Core Items are provided in the Appendix.

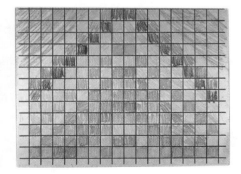

The planning activities — which entail creating individual Portfolios, deciding how and where to store portfolios, preparing work folders, and planning Core Items — should be completed before the beginning of the school year. The next step in the process is collecting work in an ongoing manner.

Collecting Work

In any given day students may write, draw, listen to an audiotape, converse, do mathematics problems, read, make a diorama, dance, build with blocks, watch a video, explore at the sand or water table, sing, play games, or interact in the dramatic play area. Some of these activities do not result in the creation of Portfolio items without intervention by the teacher. This is frequently the case in preschool and kindergarten classrooms. When process rather than product is the focus of learning, the teacher must play a more active role in documenting learning in order to include it in the Portfolio. S/he may photograph a block structure, take dictation, draw a picture of a pattern-block design, or write descriptive notes about a child's creative dance. Even with older children, teachers can help children represent their learning process.

Teachers have found many ways to represent, and help children represent, learning. Some teachers have created worksheets that allow children to draw the results of their mathematical work with manipulatives (Figure 10).

Others have prepared pre-cut paper shapes that replicate pattern blocks for children to recreate their solutions to problems involving patterning, fractions, or symmetry (Figure 11).

FIGURE 10 (LEFT)
A second grade teacher's form to reproduce geoboard designs

FIGURE 11 (RIGHT)
A second grade teacher's form to recreate a child's understanding of fractions

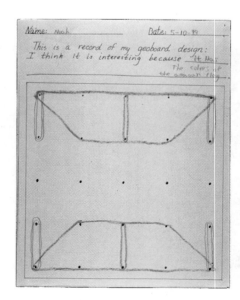

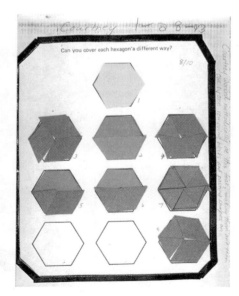

Teachers have also designed a variety of ways to help children represent their scientific investigations. Two are pictured in Figures 12 and 13.

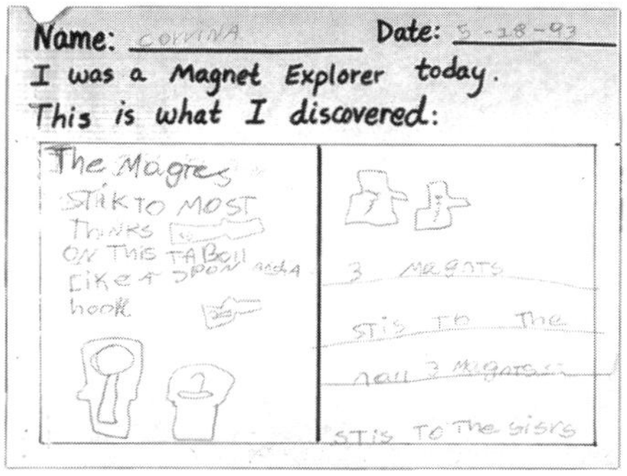

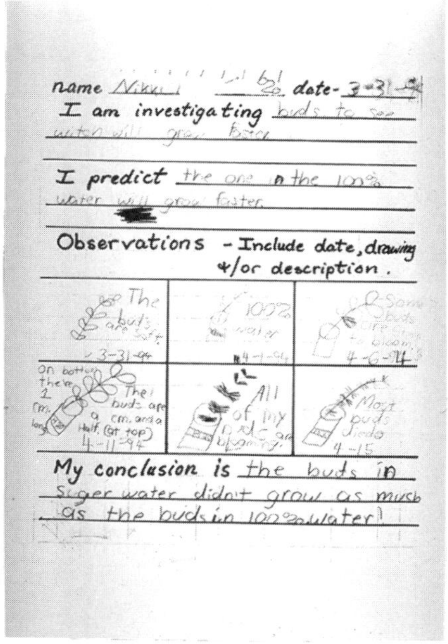

FIGURE 12 (LEFT)
Form to record magnet exploration — first grade

FIGURE 13 (RIGHT)
Form to represent the investigation process (predicting, observing, and concluding) — third grade

Still other teachers have set up opportunities for children to represent their learning during play. During a study of hospitals, the dramatic play area in a kindergarten classroom became a hospital. Here is how one child "wrote" a prescription. Note how this child's spontaneous actions demonstrate her use of letter strings (Figure 14).

FIGURE 14
Representation of a child's emergent writing during dramatic play

Photographs, audio tapes, and videotapes enrich the Portfolio Collection Process. However, the cost and practicality of these forms of documentation must be considered before using them. Photographs provide more information when accompanied by a note that describes the picture. A teacher's anecdotal notes describing something a child is doing are also appropriate when they capture a moment in the same manner as a photograph and create "word pictures." Figure 15 shows a teacher-made master. At the time the photo is taken, the teacher records the child's name, the date, and a brief description of the activity as well as the reason she took the photograph.

FIGURE 15
Teacher-created form for photographs and anecdotal records

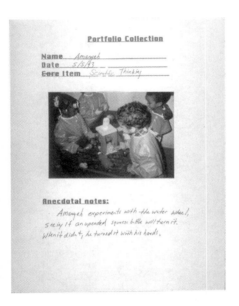

DOCUMENTATION As children complete work, they store it in their work folders or other place designated for work that will be considered for inclusion in the portfolio. *Every item in the Portfolio should be dated.* This allows teachers to compare work from different time periods in order to note and evaluate progress. Some teachers use date stamps for this purpose by placing the date stamp next to work folders and asking students to date their work before storing it.

In order to enhance the meaning of the work and to refresh teachers' and students' memories when it is time for review and selection, the teacher or student should document how the work was done. The Work Sampling System provides **PORTFOLIO ITEM RECORD** Post-it™ notes that may be placed on each sample of work (Figure 16). They allow teachers to indicate whether it is a Core or Individualized Item, and to note in which domain(s) it belongs. Other teacher-designed methods of documentation may also be used.

FIGURE 16
Portfolio Item Record
Post-it™ note

Describing how work samples are created by means of these notes is extremely informative to all who review the Portfolio. Understanding what the student was asked to do will influence how the work is evaluated later. Documentation may include comments about:

- the circumstances in which the sample was created;

- whether the activity was teacher- or child-initiated;

- whether the sample is a first, intermediate, or final draft;

- the child's familiarity with the task;

- the extent to which the work met assignment requirements;

- how the work was accomplished: independently, with peers, or with adult guidance;

- the degree of effort involved;

- the degree of organization or attention to detail;

- how the work reveals the child's approach to learning.

Figures 17 – 20 show children's work with various types of accompanying notes added by the teacher when the work was collected.

FIGURE 17
A preschool teacher's comments add information to the photo

Janet experiments with painting at the easel - making circles.

FIGURE 18
Another preschool teacher uses index cards to explain children's work

Emily   Mathematical
Winter Collection (2-99)   Thinking

In making her chain of girls, Emily decided to dress them all the same. But how would she do it? Instead of using one color and doing them all at one time, she finished the first one, then copied it one after the other.
(Notice the black lines of the penheads!)

FIGURE 19
A kindergarten teacher uses words and a picture to enhance the information given in the photo

Comments:

At first, she tried to build this structure. When it wouldn't stand, she decided to add center support

FIGURE 20
A first grade teacher's interview notes add meaning to a Portfolio item

Comments:

The Arts Core Item, Winter Watercolor Painting to Kronos Quartet: Pieces of Africa

Interview —
What did the music make you think about? Or how did it make you feel?

"Feeling sad, thinking about how my grandpa died"

To increase efficiency, some teachers create and duplicate explanatory sheets that describe learning activities and what to look for in the resulting work. This explanation is attached to the work samples (Figures 21 and 22). The activity description will be informative to family members, whether or not the work is eventually included in the Portfolio or sent home.

FIGURE 21 (LEFT)
FIGURE 22 (RIGHT)
Teacher-created activity
descriptions

_____ wrote a story in his/her "sloppy copy" writing book, and then conferenced with a friend and/or the teacher about it.

Next, editing and revisions were done, also in the sloppy copy book.

Then he/she typed the story up on the word processor (copy #1), and made other last changes (copy #2).

Last of all, a teacher made final corrections on the computer and made the final draft printout.

Your child's writing is an excellent way to chart his/her growth and progress.

Look for growth in —
• Letter/sound knowledge
• Spaces between words
• Use of lower-case letters (children begin by using all upper-case letters).

In second grade, children begin to use punctuation, but not consistently. You should begin to see some use of periods and capitals.

The content of writing changes as well, moving from simple sentences to more descriptive sentences. The child's stories become more elaborate as s/he develops writing skills. In many cases you can almost begin to see your child's personality emerge in the writing through the words and phrases s/he uses.

Selecting Work

Periodically, the teacher and child review collected work in order to select examples for the Portfolio. Making selections of work for the Portfolio is an activity that may be done by teachers, by teachers with children, and by children alone with guidance from teachers. The decision about how much to involve children in the selection process rests with individual teachers. Striving for child involvement is valuable because it allows children to feel ownership of their learning and their Portfolios. It also provides opportunities for them to reflect on their work and think critically about criteria for evaluation. The following section about selecting work samples assumes the involvement of children.

Five issues should be considered as teachers plan and organize the process of selecting work. They are:

1 Selecting samples of work for Core Items;

2 Selecting samples of work for Individualized Items;

3 Creating a routine for selection;

4 Establishing criteria for selection of work; and

5 Documenting work that has been selected for the Portfolio.

SELECTING SAMPLES OF WORK FOR CORE ITEMS Work samples selected as Core Items should be chosen because they represent children's typical work in that area of learning. The work should also reflect each child's individuality. As stated earlier, an implicit assumption of Work Sampling is that children have different approaches to learning and, therefore, reveal their skills and knowledge in many different ways. A talented artist may represent learning in Social Studies through drawing, while a strong writer represents it in prose. In Work Sampling, Core Items reflect the same learning area, but actual work may be different from child to child.

The CORE ITEM COLLECTION PLAN form (Figure 23) has been designed to help teachers keep track of Core Item collection. It is placed in the front of the Portfolio and serves as a table of contents for Core Items in the Portfolio. After the teacher lists the Core Items, s/he copies the sheet for each child's Portfolio. As work is selected, s/he checks off the appropriate collection period.

FIGURE 23
Core Item Collection Plan form

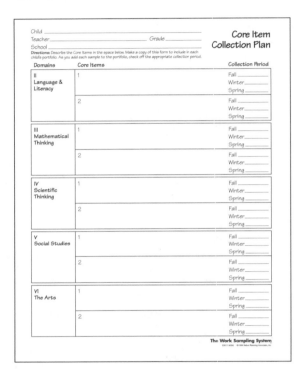

Some teachers post a grid for each collection period listing Core Items at the top of the page and students' names in a column on the left side (Figure 24). As Core Items are collected, teachers check appropriate boxes to keep track of which items still need to be collected.

FIGURE 24
Core Item collection tally sheet helps keep track of items still to be collected

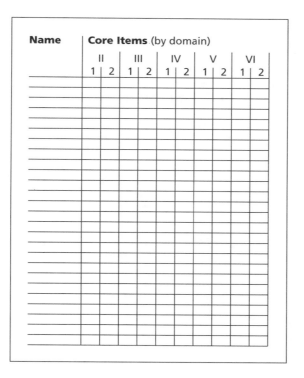

Name	Core Items (by domain)									
	II		III		IV		V		VI	
	1	2	1	2	1	2	1	2	1	2

SELECTING SAMPLES OF WORK FOR INDIVIDUALIZED ITEMS Samples of work that are the child's "best work," or represent a significant accomplishment, are included as Individualized Items. A teacher or child may choose to include an example of work that represents a departure from the student's usual way of working. Individualized Items may be selected spontaneously at any time during the collection period, and these selections may also be revised or exchanged until the end of a collection period.

When selecting Individualized Items, look for work that elaborates the portrait of a child's learning process. Individualized Items are intended to capture unique characteristics of a child and reflect learning that integrates several domains. Select work that:

■ **Represents a child's special interests.** Work may be included that represents the child's continued interest in a field of study; for example, animals, space exploration, vehicles, or sports.

■ **Illustrates the child's approach to learning.** The items may feature media in which a child likes to work, a child's tendency to focus on details, or a child's preference for framing an inquiry in the context of a larger issue.

■ **Represents the child's "best work".** Work that may not be typical but represents a child's best effort may be included as an Individualized Item.

■ **Represents specific accomplishments.** Samples of work are chosen to represent significant moments in the child's learning, such as the first finger-painting by a child who had previously avoided messy activities, a graph the child worked diligently to create, or a piece of writing that shows the child's experimentation with a new genre.

■ **Shows the integration of several domains.** Items may be included to demonstrate how the child integrates skills from several domains. For example, a representation of a science experience in which the child wrote, painted, tallied, and drew conclusions about an investigation, might be included as an Individualized Item.

SUMMARY OF CORE ITEM AND INDIVIDUALIZED ITEM COLLECTION

	Core Items	Individualized Items
Major Functions	• Representative work in five domains • Progress in five domains	• Unique characteristics of child • Integrated learning from multiple domains
Planning	• Teacher plans in advance	• Spontaneous
Relation to Domains	• Five domains represented	• Work may show integration of learning from several domains, but is not linked directly to a single domain
Collection Period	• Same area of learning for each collection period	• Items vary per collection period
Total Number	• 2 for each of 5 domains, 3 times per year; total = 30	• Minimum of 5 during each collection period, 3 times per year; total = 15

ESTABLISHING A ROUTINE Regardless of whether teachers involve students or make selections independently, it is necessary to establish a routine for work selection. When teachers wait until the end of the collection period to make selections, they may find they do not have enough examples of work from which to choose. Or, the task may be very cumbersome because the stack of work to review is very large. Getting organized for work selection with children requires making two decisions: how often work will be selected and how children will be grouped.

How often? With young children, teachers review work at least once each week. Given the short attention spans of young children, their tendency to want to take work home immediately, and their difficulty reviewing many samples at once, a weekly schedule is usually the most manageable. This schedule may be used with older students as well. However, it is also possible to review work less frequently with older students, possibly once every two or three weeks.

How many in a group? In many classrooms, Portfolio review and selection involves the entire class. These review sessions generally begin with a discussion about how to make selections (see below for ideas on selection criteria). Children work individually, with a partner, or in small groups, and the teacher circulates and converses with the children. Another strategy is to hold individual or group conferences while the rest of the class reviews their Portfolios independently or with peers. Children may be encouraged to discuss their choices with one another. Many teachers try to schedule this time when an adult volunteer, family member, student teacher, paraprofessional, older student, or other helper is present. Helpers can assist students with the selection and documentation of work. The less familiarity children have with the process of selecting work, the more adult assistance they will need.

CRITERIA FOR SELECTION OF ITEMS Teachers use many criteria for the selection of work samples. Some criteria reflect the students' efforts or progress ("select work that shows what you are learning about plant growth"). Other criteria are tied closely to specific standards for a particular kind of work ("select a story with a clearly described setting and a conflict that gets resolved"; "choose a scientific investigation in which you made a prediction, tested it, and drew a conclusion"). When children are making selections, they will inevitably need guidance about how to make decisions. In the discussions that precede review sessions, teachers can offer children one or two guidelines for selecting work. Teachers may ask children to select:

- something that was really enjoyable to do;

- something that shows how much they are learning;

- work that was hard;

- something that shows their use of descriptive language;

- work that shows at least two strategies that they used to solve a math problem;

- something they would like to do again;

- a piece of writing that reminds them of a story read or heard;

- something they wrote that describes an important observation they made;

- a painting where they blended colors in a way that they really liked.

Once children gain familiarity with criteria for selection, they will begin to develop their own criteria.

Conversations about selection criteria between teachers and students, and between students and their peers, provide the basis for the development of the child's personal standards for selection and self-evaluation. When children first begin making selections, their reasons for doing so are likely to be quite simplistic or uninformative. Comments such as

"Because I like it" or "I don't know" are to be expected. By engaging in the selection process, children learn to evaluate themselves and begin to take increased responsibility for their own learning. Experience and discussion are very important for children to become skilled at this endeavor.

DOCUMENTATION IS ESSENTIAL The reason for selection should be included in the documentation on the selected work sample. In addition to stating the criteria for selection, other documentation of work may take place during the selection process. Children can describe the assignment and the process involved in doing the task. They can reflect on their efforts and accomplishments. Children can consider why the selection is a meaningful contribution to the Portfolio. When children are old enough to do this recording on their own, the documentation itself becomes an important part of the Item. With young children, teachers should try to have realistic expectations about how much to document, since children cannot take on much of this effort themselves.

Children's work is formally reviewed and evaluated three times during the year. Until then, teachers and students may decide to change items previously included in the Portfolio. Each review includes evaluation of performance during the collection period and progress from one collection period to the next.

Evaluating the Portfolio

Evaluating the Portfolio involves two processes: evaluation of Core and Individualized Items, and evaluation of the entire Portfolio for the Summary Report. The second type of evaluation is discussed in the Summary Report chapter (see Chapter 4).

Assessment of the Portfolio is guided by developmental expectations. Critical to this process is the teacher's specification of his/her standards of performance and progress. Once the teacher has delineated grade-level or classroom expectations, the student's work is compared to those standards. Some relevant considerations include:

- How does the work meet these expectations?

- Where specifically does it fall short of these expectations?

- Which specific features of the work show emerging skill?

- What kind of work would be considered advanced for children of this age?

- Which areas need continued observation?

When a teacher evaluates a child's performance as represented in the Portfolio s/he examines individual samples. Although looking at one item may bring to mind other items, a single item should never be used to evaluate the totality of a child's work in a particular domain. A single item only provides one piece of the picture and should be evaluated and weighed against other information.

EVALUATION OF CORE ITEMS Work selected as Core Items is evaluated only for the learning represented in the specified domain. For example, a Scientific Thinking Core Item should be judged only for the child's scientific thinking (for example, skills of observation, prediction, and explanation) even if it also reveals a child's fine motor abilities or artistic expression.

Figures 25 and 26 show two examples (fall and spring) from a kindergartner's journal. They represent a Core Item in the domain of Language and Literacy — a sample of a child's writing.

FIGURE 25 (LEFT)
FIGURE 26 (RIGHT)
A kindergartner's fall and spring Core Items in Language and Literacy

Comments:

Beginning to use phonetic spelling. Computers — a frequent writing topic.

Comments:

Mike worked carefully and independently on his journal today.

Example 3 represents Mike's teacher's evaluation of the fall work (these evaluation examples represent the teacher's thought process and need not be in written form).

EXAMPLE 3
Mike used a beginning sound per word, demonstrating his understanding of letter-sound correspondence. The writing represents a complete thought, and is related to the illustration. This entry shows that Mike's writing meets or exceeds my expectations for a kindergartner at this time of year.

Mike's teacher would then look at all other examples of writing in his portfolio to see if they are consistent with this one. She would also examine his other Language and Literacy Core Item, and the Individualized Items that provide information about Mike's development in Language and Literacy, in order to rate his performance in this domain.

Example 4 shows Mike's teacher's comments about the spring sample.

EXAMPLE 4

I notice that Mike used some conventional spellings in familiar words. He used phonetic spelling for other words with fair success. Mike is beginning to understand how to write separate words, and he divided them with a vertical line. He composed two full sentences to represent his thoughts. His work shows that his writing is what I would expect (or more) from a kindergartner at this time of year.

When I compare this entry to the one in the fall, I see that Mike has grown in his understanding of letter-sound correspondence, using more letters to portray beginning, middle, and ending sounds in his writing. His writing now includes more than one thought at a time. Mike's fall and spring journal entries demonstrate his progress in writing.

Mike's teacher will use the information from all of the work samples in Language and Literacy (Core and Individualized Items from spring) to rate Mike's current level of performance in this domain. She will review all his work in this domain from all three collection periods, in addition to reviewing the information in the Checklist, to determine her evaluation of Mike's overall progress in Language and Literacy.

Figures 27 and 28 show a third grader's representation of the use of strategies to solve problems involving number.

FIGURE 27 (LEFT)
FIGURE 28 (RIGHT)
A third grader's fall and spring Core Items in Mathematical Thinking

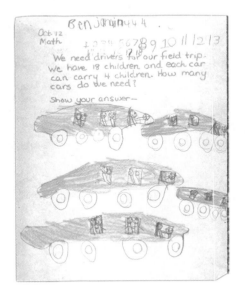

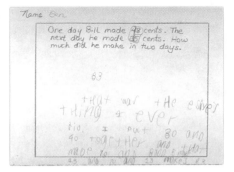

Comments:

Worked independently. Used drawing and counting — shared strategy with the rest of the class.

Comments:

Ben worked quickly but with great concentration. Helped a friend who needed assistance with this problem.

During review of Ben's portfolio to complete the fall Summary Report, Ben's teacher commented (Example 5):

EXAMPLE 5   *Ben solved the problem correctly. He used drawing and counting-on to solve this problem, and used numerical symbols only to count the number of passengers. Ben's work in solving this problem shows that he uses the strategies I would expect of a second grader in the fall.*

Ben's teacher reviewed his Core Item only for the work it was meant to represent. She was careful not to be influenced by the quality of his drawing, by the fact that his coloring strayed out of the lines, or by how Ben cleverly drew the steering wheels and drivers. These insights into Ben's work are not relevant to the evaluation of his mathematical thinking, although they do provide information about the overall quality of his thinking and his work. The teacher will also review the other Core and Individualized Items before rating Ben's performance in the domain as a whole.

During review of Ben's portfolio to complete the spring Summary Report, Ben's teacher commented (Example 6):

EXAMPLE 6   *Ben used mental addition or computation to solve this problem. He shows an understanding of place value, and seemed to use regrouping in his addition. His work on this problem indicates that he has an age/grade-appropriate grasp of the use of strategies to solve numerical problems.*

When I compare the fall and the winter Core Items, I can see growth in Ben's use of strategies to solve problems involving number. Ben's use of mental addition and computation in the spring are more sophisticated than his use of counting-on in the fall. Additionally, his representation of the mathematical process that he used is more symbolic and less concrete. He was able to describe the way he solved the problem in words, and demonstrated confidence in solving the problem and describing his solution. The changes in Ben's use of strategies, and his ability to apply strategies to solve a more complicated mathematical problem, show that Ben has made the kind of progress I would expect of a third grader during one school year.

Note that Ben's teacher did not assess his handwriting, or respond to the writing skills demonstrated in Ben's work. The teacher evaluated only those aspects of the work that inform her about Ben's use of strategies to solve problems. The teacher will review the other Core Items and the Individualized Items, as well as the Checklist, to make an evaluation of Ben's overall progress.

EVALUATION OF INDIVIDUALIZED ITEMS When evaluating Individualized Items, multiple aspects of the work (that is, information relevant to many different domains) should be assessed and can contribute to the teacher's understanding of the student's work. Figure 29 shows an Individualized Item from a first grader, and the teacher's discussion of what she learned from this work.

FIGURE 29

A first grader's Individualized Item (journal entry) that illustrates integrated learning and a specific accomplishment

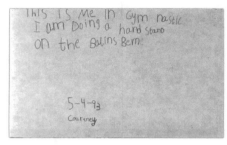

Comments:

Courtney said, "I want this in my portfolio because I've been practicing and practicing doing a handstand like this, and this is the day after I finally did it."

When reviewing Courtney's Portfolio for the spring Summary Report, the teacher noted (Example 7):

EXAMPLE 7

It's good that Courtney decided to keep the writing and the illustration together. I learn more from viewing the text and the art side by side. Her achievement of a physical skill (Physical Development), and her sense of accomplishment (Personal and Social Development) are clear. Courtney's reason for including this work in her portfolio also indicates her sustained interest and persistence in the face of frustration (Personal and Social Development).

Courtney used a mix of conventional and invented spelling, as well as a mix of upper and lower case letters. She used no punctuation, but the words are well spaced. She was able to communicate clear and complete thoughts (Language and Literacy).

Courtney's picture shows her ability to express both ideas and emotion in drawing. In depicting her gymnastics class she used perspective and balance in her composition. She shows attention to detail by including many pieces of gymnastic equipment in the drawing. Her sense of accomplishment is shown in the smiling figure and heart she drew to represent herself (The Arts).

Courtney's teacher attends to all the information in the work in order to learn about Courtney's development in many domains. As she reviews the other portfolio items to rate Courtney's performance in different domains, she will take what she has learned from this work into account.

This journal entry will also figure into the teacher's assessment of Courtney's progress in different domains.

NEXT STEPS AFTER EVALUATION After teachers evaluate a child's Portfolio work, they should consider whether anything has been added to their understanding of the child. Evaluating a student's work may confirm or change the teacher's working hypothesis about an individual child. A discrepancy between the teacher's prior assessment and evaluation of the current work highlights the need for continued evaluation of the child's work.

The teacher completes her evaluation by deciding whether some action needs to be taken as a result of the information acquired. In other words, evaluation is not the final step in the process. Rather, it identifies an opportunity for further teacher intervention designed to support the student's learning. The teacher may want to think about what steps to take next and how to incorporate the information gathered from the portfolio into curriculum and instructional planning.

Frequently Asked Questions about Portfolio Collection

Q *What do I need to begin Portfolio collection?*

A To ensure a smooth start to Portfolio collection, it is important that you have supplies ready before the beginning of the school year. This includes the materials to create a Portfolio for each child, storage bins, and work folders.

Next, you should plan Core Items. This entails deciding on two areas of learning for each of the five Core Item domains. Each area of learning should be written on the Core Item Collection Plan Sheet and reproduced in enough copies to put one in the front of each child's Portfolio. At this point, you are ready to begin collecting children's work.

Q *I prefer a different way to create my students' Portfolios. Is there anything special about the ways described in this chapter?*

A The suggestions included in this chapter are not intended to be a prescription for the definitive way to create Portfolios or collect work. Rather, they are proposed as suggestions and a jumping-off point for teachers to develop their own ideas and practices. Because you know about the resources available to you, you are in the best position to make these decisions (how to create Portfolios, how to prepare work folders, how often to make Portfolio selections). What is essential is the systematic collection of two kinds of work: Core Items and Individualized Items.

Q *Should all work go into work folders?*

A At the beginning of the year, it is probably a good idea for most work to be saved in work folders. As you and your students become more familiar with Portfolio collection, you may decide that some kinds of work should go home immediately. In general, it is important to save work that is most informative about the child's learning.

Work samples are informative when they reveal multiple aspects of childrens' learning, thinking, and performance. For example, journal entries provide information about the child's ability to express ideas, organize written text, apply conventions of print (spacing, capitalization, punctuation), spell, and use vocabulary. They also provide a window into the child's personal and social development by revealing the child's interests, motivations, daily life events, style of thinking, domain-related knowledge, attitudes, etc. In contrast, a work sheet that requires the child to read a passage of text and to apply rules of capitalization sheds light only on the child's ability to capitalize correctly. Portfolio items should be broad rather than narrow and should be designed in such a way that they place few limits on what may be learned.

Q *Should I keep my notes about students in their Portfolio?*

A Portfolios are intended to contain only the children's work. This is not the place to keep Checklists, your observation notes, or notes to and from home. For each child there should be another file in which your memos and notes, Checklists, and copies of Summary Reports are kept. These can be stored in a file cabinet because they are not expected to be made available to children.

Q *I'm a preschool teacher, and I feel that it is very important to document growth in Personal and Social Development, and Physical Development. Why aren't they included as domains for the collection of Core Items?*

A These two domains have not been designated as Core Item domains because children's work in these two areas does not lend itself to the creation of products to include in the Portfolio. For example, products do not generally result from gross motor activities or from dramatic play. Assessment of these domains requires anecdotal note-taking and greater teacher involvement.

Personal and Social Development and Physical Development are extremely important domains. However, in order to keep the workload manageable, they are documented solely through teacher observations on the Developmental Checklists.

If you decide that you want to collect Core Items in these domains, and are willing to spend the additional time, you should do so. Such Portfolios will contain a higher proportion of anecdotal notes in these domains than for the other domains.

Q *If the entire class has the same Core Items in each domain, won't all the portfolios contain children's responses to the same projects or assignments?*

A Children's Portfolios will not all contain representations of the same projects because Portfolio items are collected in an ongoing way during the course of each collection period and because they are based on learning that occurs on more than one occasion in the classroom. Consider this illustration:

Science Core Item: A record of children's observation and description of natural phenomena.

Activities in the fall include:

- Collecting, observing, and drawing leaves
- Observing and recording the habits of the class pet
- Observing and charting the foods eaten by the class pet
- Observing and drawing growth of seeds

Children in this class have many opportunities to observe and describe natural phenomena. The sample selected for each child will depend on the child's interest in the activity and the quality of his/her work. Because there have been many opportunities for children to observe and describe, this area of learning will be represented in different ways in children's portfolios.

Portfolio samples are most successful when they are easy to collect. This means that the work should occur frequently in the classroom rather than being contrived for the sole purpose of producing a Core Item. If children write text daily or even weekly, many samples will be available for inclusion in the Portfolio. The more opportunities for such work, the less likely an absence or schedule change will disrupt Portfolio collection.

Q *Should work that is included in the Portfolio be graded?*

A Students' work should not receive a grade. Your comments on students' work are most valuable when they help students reflect on their efforts and progress. When work in the Portfolio is graded in conventional ways (for example, a number or letter grade), the grade becomes the focus rather than the work.

Q *How do I integrate Portfolio collection into my existing curriculum and classroom schedule?*

A To ensure the best fit between Portfolio collection and your classroom, think about Portfolio collection as you plan each week. Some teachers list their Core Items in their plan book. As you review your curriculum plans, consider purposeful activities and the types of representations children might create (such as writings, drawings, maps, models, dictations, charts, and graphs).

Many teachers do not realize that what they already do is appropriate for Portfolio collection. Usually you do not need to plan special or different learning activities for children; you only need to plan and collect them differently. Because you choose areas of learning from curriculum that are important to you, Core Items arise from the ongoing activities of the classroom.

Q *How can I involve specialists in the Portfolio process?*

A Portfolio collection can be greatly enriched when classroom teachers and specialists collaborate. Specialists provide many opportunities for children to create products that document learning. In addition, specialists and resource teachers can support classroom themes and units by planning related activities in the special subject area. Collaboration between classroom teachers and specialists broadens the range of materials and media that children may include in their Portfolios. (For further discussion of these issues, see page 121.)

Q *How can I find time to file the children's work?*

A Many teachers find it most efficient to file work in the Portfolio regularly and frequently. This avoids large piles of work that need to be filed at the end of the collection period. Some teachers rely on parent volunteers to help with the filing and general management tasks associated with Portfolio collection. Older children can assume many of the management tasks themselves.

Q *What happens to Portfolios at the end of the year?*

A Individual schools or districts make this decision. An important factor to remember is that Portfolios are collections of children's work and belong to the children. Therefore, most of the work eventually goes home with the student at the end of the year or at the beginning of the next year.

Some schools have developed their own year-end strategies. Some create a cumulative school Portfolio for each child by keeping one Core Item from one or two domains from the final collection period each year. Sometimes, teachers also decide to keep several items from the fall collection during the child's first year of school to illustrate the child's entering performance. After items are selected for the next year's teacher or for a cumulative school Portfolio, the major part of the Portfolio is sent home with children.

Q *Should I show the Portfolio to the child's new teacher before sending it home?*

A The Portfolio collection process can help children and teachers make the transition from one grade to the next. Part of the transition process involves reflecting on the year's learning. At the end of the school year, you can ask students to review their entire portfolio. Through reviewing their Portfolio, and with your guidance, children will be able to observe their own growth and development.

A second part of the transition process is getting acquainted with the new teacher. Instead of grades or "cumulative records," the Portfolio can be used as a way for teachers to get to know their new students. After reviewing the year's work, you might suggest selecting two or three items to keep at school to show the child's new teacher in the fall. With the aid of the Portfolios, either in whole or in part, children can introduce themselves to their new teacher, showing their work and expressing their own reflections and observations. The new teacher will have an opportunity to begin the dialogue with individual children about important learning experiences to anticipate during the coming year. After the Portfolio conference in the fall, the child may take his/her Portfolio home.

Q *How will Portfolio assessment influence my curriculum and instruction?*

A Reviewing children's work provides an opportunity for you to monitor individual students' work. As you carefully study children's work, you learn about your students as learners and as people, their work habits, personal styles, thought processes, accomplishments, strengths, and difficulties. For example, after reviewing a portfolio, you may notice that one student consistently makes elaborate drawings, sketches, and paintings. With this knowledge, you can begin to consider ways to involve this student in learning through art, to reinforce his strengths, and to show him the connection between the visual arts and other domains of learning. Another teacher may observe that a child comprehends story structure but has difficulty representing this understanding because of weak fine motor skills. She may suggest that the child recite the story into a tape recorder. In this way the child experiences success, and the teacher has a more accurate representation of the child's understanding of story structure. By studying children's work over time, you can observe their strengths and the kinds of tasks that cause difficulty.

Also, you gain perspective on how your students are responding to instructional activities. You might notice, for example, that the graphing activity was too complicated for children, and that most children understood less about graphing than expected. As a result, you may decide to engage children in additional, less-complex graphing experiences. Another teacher may see that students' work folders are full of examples of social studies topics but less often include scientific thinking. This may indicate that very limited opportunities for scientific investigation occur in the classroom.

Further Discussion about the Portfolio Collection Process

Involving Children in the Portfolio Collection Process

INTRODUCING PORTFOLIOS TO CHILDREN The first step in involving children in the Portfolio Collection Process is to talk with them about Portfolios. Children need the same kind of explanation about Portfolios that they would about any other new material or procedure in the classroom. Teachers should begin by explaining what a Portfolio is, why it is being kept, and what the child's role is. It may be helpful to talk with children about people who keep portfolios and the reasons they use portfolios in their work. Family members may be artists, photographers, or journalists and have a portfolio they could share with the class. Talking about how portfolios are used and how to choose work to include helps students begin to see Portfolios as a meaningful part of classroom work.

Portfolio collection invites students into the assessment process by involving them in:

- filing and dating work

- reviewing and selecting work

- evaluating their own performance and progress

FILING AND DATING WORK Children can help with many of the management tasks associated with Portfolio collection. Depending on their age, they may be able to:

- date work

- complete Portfolio Item Record Post-it notes

- file work

REVIEWING AND SELECTING WORK The more experienced students are with Portfolio collection, the better they are at review, selection, and evaluation. Regardless of the child's age, lack of prior experience with Portfolios will mean that the explanations they offer for work selections are simple. They may say, "because I like it," or "because it's neat." And their thoughts about their Portfolios may be superficial at first: "I like it," or "I wrote a lot." It is the teacher's responsibility to develop children's Portfolio evaluation skills.

For students, reviewing work provides an opportunity to reflect on what has been occurring in the classroom and what they have been doing and learning. Looking at work reminds students of the experiences that led to the creation of the work. Reviewing their work helps children see the changes they have made since the beginning of the year and develop a sense for how much they have grown. Review is also an opportunity to notice where the work is weak, and to motivate revision. In making choices for Portfolio inclusion, children have an opportunity to express their thinking about their work and what it means to them.

Involving children in the Portfolio collection process means teaching them about criteria for making choices and guiding them in making judgments about their own work. Selecting items for the Portfolio is a first step. Even very young children can be involved meaningfully in this process. Children's first attempts may not appear very successful. Time and practice gradually yield success.

For example, one teacher established two folders for each child, one marked "easy" and the other "hard." To obtain Individualized Items, every Friday she gave the students their collected work (all the work they produced that week) and asked them to put something in each of the folders. The rest of the work went home with the child. This encouraged children to become involved in reviewing their own work and thinking about what they are able to do. It also assisted them in noticing their own progress as the "hard" tasks become "easy" over time.

The Work Sampling System includes a reproducible form that specifically addresses the child's reflection on his/her work. Entitled "THOUGHTS ABOUT MY PORTFOLIO," the sheet provides a place for the student's name, and room for the student to write or dictate comments (Figure 30). One copy of the form is used for each collection period. Some teachers use this form, or one similar to it, as an opportunity to conference with students about their work at the end of each collection period. These conferences provide opportunities for students to set goals for themselves, make plans with the teacher for working toward new goals, and evaluating their progress. Figures 31 – 33 show children's evaluations of their own Portfolios.

FIGURE 30
Thoughts About My
Portfolio form

FIGURE 31 (LEFT)
FIGURE 32 (RIGHT)
Children's evaluations of
their own work and
Portfolios — first grade and
third grade

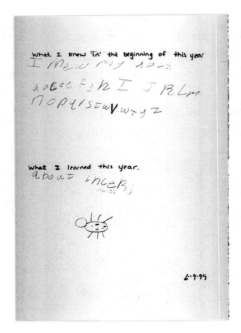

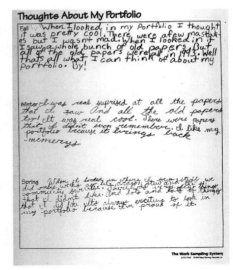

FIGURE 33
A fourth grader's self-evaluation

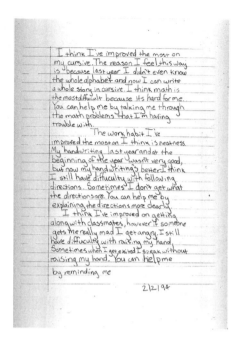

Using Portfolios with Children of Different Ages

PRESCHOOL Self-evaluation is a learned skill, a capability developed through experience and guidance. Preschoolers are generally not very reflective. In preschool, the act of reviewing the Portfolio will likely be the most relevant to children. Children can be introduced to the idea of having a collection of their work, and can feel great satisfaction in reviewing their work and seeing their growth. As children grow, their role in the design and selection of the Portfolio grows with them.

Three year olds should not be expected to make meaningful choices of work for their Portfolio. Frequently, items in the Portfolio may be teacher notes that are not meaningful to preschoolers. Occasionally, teachers may provide opportunities for older preschool children to make choices. These children will only be asked to select one item from a group of three or four. For example, the teacher might say to a child, "I see you made three paintings with finger paint this week. Which one of these would you like to put in your Portfolio?" The teacher might also ask children why they chose the one they did and talk with them about their choice. At this age, children's comments about why they made their choice and what they like about it may not be deeply reflective or informative.

KINDERGARTEN In addition to reviewing the work and remembering experiences, learning to make choices can be a focused activity of Portfolio review at this age. Within clearly defined limits, kindergarten children can begin to make choices about the work they want included in their Portfolio. Teachers may provide criteria for making choices such as deciding between hard and easy tasks, or selecting something to work on again or to try for the first time. More open-ended choices may be possible from a small collection of work, such as choosing something that shows how the child writes or draws and saying why; choosing the painting the child likes most; or selecting the pattern the child finds most interesting. Topics of informal conversation in the classroom might address why children made certain choices, why some work was fun to create, what else they would like to learn, etc. Review of the Portfolio will be helpful in transition at the end of the year, and can begin to focus the child's sense of his/her own growth.

FIRST AND SECOND GRADE Children at this age are continuing to learn to review their work and make choices of items to include in the Portfolio. A prompt that could be introduced after initial experience with Portfolio review and selection might be, "Choose the journal entry that shows the most about the way you write." Or, the teacher might pose a question more specifically to address work in areas of core learning: "What would you choose to show how you solve mathematical problems?"

As children become older, they begin to evaluate their work more carefully. First and second graders begin to talk about what constitutes good work. Some questions that help students engage in evaluation of individual samples of work are:

- What did you learn from this work?

- What do you want to know more about in this area?

- Where do you feel you have shown the most progress?

THIRD THROUGH FIFTH GRADE Children this age begin to set goals in their learning and can review their progress toward goals. They can answer questions about their Portfolios:

- How did you choose the work in the Portfolio?

- What does your work show about you as a learner?

- What are some things you can do well, and what are things you still want to work on?

Or they may be asked to comment on individual items by answering questions such as:

- Why did you select this sample?

- What do you see as the strengths of this item?

- What was especially important to you when you were working on this?

- What did you struggle with?

- If you could work on this more, what would you do?

- How is this the same or different from your other work?

- What does this work show about you as a writer, scientist, mathematician, or artist?

As children become more capable of reflection, evaluation, and setting goals and working toward them, their role in the Portfolio process expands. However, it is also important not to overdo this aspect of classroom life. Most learning is for its own sake and not for the purpose of documentation. When students are asked to respond to every activity formally, by writing, drawing, or other expression, they can grow tired of the demand and lose their enthusiasm for the work itself.

Family Involvement

As Portfolio collection becomes central to the classroom, it also becomes an important vehicle for sharing classroom life with families. Some schools sponsor Portfolio Nights when parents are invited to school with their children to review their Portfolios. In other schools, family members are invited to come in at their convenience and look through the Portfolios with their child.

For many teachers, the Portfolio provides the central focus for the family-teacher conference. Teachers may illustrate their comments on the Summary Report with work from children's Portfolios. They may also share the children's reasons for including items in the Portfolios with their families.

Children can also be involved in family-teacher conferences, using their Portfolios as the basis to illustrate their efforts, progress, and achievements. This enables parents and teachers to support children through the recognition of well-done work and in planning goals for children. Some teachers conduct Portfolio Conferences with children before family-teacher conferences and share the information they will be discussing with the parents.

Conclusion

The Work Sampling System Portfolio process is designed to organize the collection of children's work and make it manageable for teachers and students to document the breadth of children's growth. The structure of the Portfolio system enables teacher and students to create Portfolios that demonstrate:

- the quality of children's work;

- their progress throughout the year;

- students' unique characteristics; and

- learning that is integrative of many domains.

Portfolios provide an in-depth portrait of children, their work, their approach to learning, and their accomplishments. This portrait complements the information provided by the Checklists. Portfolios provide essential information about student learning and growth that supports and enriches the evaluation provided in the Summary Report.

CHAPTER 4

Summary Reports

Summarizing Performance and Progress

THIS CHAPTER ADDRESSES THE THIRD ELEMENT OF THE WORK SAMpling System — the Summary Report. The chapter is divided into four sections as follows:

- Introduction to the Summary Report

- How to Complete the Summary Report

- Frequently Asked Questions about the Summary Report

- Further Discussion about the Summary Report

Introduction to the Summary Report

Assessment involves two complementary processes: documentation and evaluation. In Work Sampling, teachers gather evidence that illustrates student performance in each of the seven Work Sampling System domains. Throughout each collection period, teachers observe students during classroom learning activities and document their observations. They also review student work as they help students make selections for inclusion in the Portfolio. These ongoing processes of documentation are fundamental to the Work Sampling System.

In addition to documentation, assessment involves evaluation, or decision-making. At the end of each collection period, teachers integrate what they have learned from the Developmental Checklists and the Portfolio Collection Process with their own knowledge of child development in order to make evaluative decisions about the student's *performance* and *progress* in each of the seven domains. They summarize their knowledge of the child as they make ratings and write a commentary describing the child's strengths and areas of concern. These evaluative decisions are recorded on the Summary Report.

Description

The Summary Report is a three-part carbonless form that is completed three times each year. It is used to communicate information about students' performance and progress to families and administrators and replaces conventional report cards.

Purpose

The Summary Report has four major purposes:

1 To provide a profile of each student's strengths and difficulties across the seven Work Sampling domains;

2 To provide families with information about student performance and progress;

3 To assist the teacher with instructional planning; and

4 To provide administrators with information about student achievement.

Features of the Summary Report

■ The Summary Report is completed by the child's teacher at the end of each collection period, three times during the school year.

■ Each Summary Report form provides three carbonless copies on pages of different colors. The top copy (white) is for the family; the second copy (yellow) is for the child's cumulative school file; and the bottom copy (pink) is for the teacher's file, to allow the teacher to refer to earlier Reports.

■ Two versions of the Summary Report are available: the standard Summary Report, and the Narrative Summary Report.

■ The standard SUMMARY REPORT form consists of three sections. On the left side of the form are ratings of performance and progress. Next to the rating columns is space for commentary. Identifying information is located on the right side of the form.

■ The NARRATIVE SUMMARY REPORT form is designed for programs that are non-graded, and for preschool programs that prefer entirely narrative reports. This reporting option expands the allotted space for commentary, but does not include the ratings for performance and progress. Programs can request the Narrative Summary Report form in place of the standard Summary Report.

■ Both versions of the Summary Report are available in Spanish.

Structure of the Standard Summary Report

Child's identifying information and attendance record

Current collection period (fall, winter, or year-end)

List of domains and components

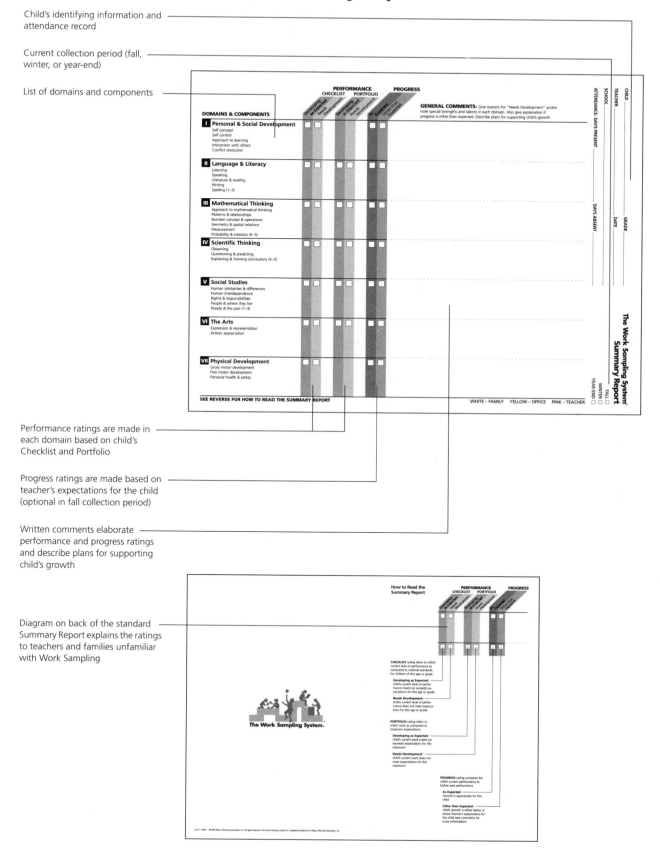

Performance ratings are made in each domain based on child's Checklist and Portfolio

Progress ratings are made based on teacher's expectations for the child (optional in fall collection period)

Written comments elaborate performance and progress ratings and describe plans for supporting child's growth

Diagram on back of the standard Summary Report explains the ratings to teachers and families unfamiliar with Work Sampling

Structure of the Narrative Summary Report

Current collection period (fall, winter, or year-end)

Child's identifying information and attendance record

List of domains and components

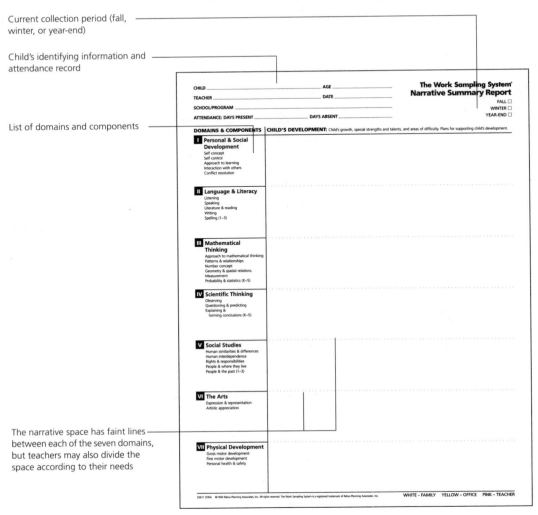

CHILD _____ AGE _____

TEACHER _____ DATE _____

SCHOOL/PROGRAM _____

ATTENDANCE: DAYS PRESENT _____ DAYS ABSENT _____

The Work Sampling System®
Narrative Summary Report

FALL ☐
WINTER ☐
YEAR-END ☐

DOMAINS & COMPONENTS | **CHILD'S DEVELOPMENT:** Child's growth, special strengths and talents, and areas of difficulty. Plans for supporting child's development.

I Personal & Social Development
Self concept
Self control
Approach to learning
Interaction with others
Conflict resolution

II Language & Literacy
Listening
Speaking
Literature & reading
Writing
Spelling (1–3)

III Mathematical Thinking
Approach to mathematical thinking
Patterns & relationships
Number concept
Geometry & spatial relations
Measurement
Probability & statistics (K–5)

IV Scientific Thinking
Observing
Questioning & predicting
Explaining & forming conclusions (K–5)

V Social Studies
Human similarities & differences
Human interdependence
Rights & responsibilities
People & where they live
People & the past (1–3)

VI The Arts
Expression & representation
Artistic appreciation

VII Physical Development
Gross motor development
Fine motor development
Personal health & safety

32611 (3/94) ©1994 Rebus Planning Associates, Inc. All rights reserved. The Work Sampling System is a registered trademark of Rebus Planning Associates, Inc.   WHITE – FAMILY   YELLOW – OFFICE   PINK – TEACHER

The narrative space has faint lines between each of the seven domains, but teachers may also divide the space according to their needs

How to Complete the Summary Report

Completing a Summary Report consists of four steps:

STEP 1   Review the information collected for each student (see page 85).

STEP 2   Evaluate and rate student performance and progress (see page 85).

STEP 3   Write a commentary for each student that describes a profile of the child's strengths and areas of concern (see page 90).

STEP 4   Share the Summary Report with the child's family (see page 99).

Each step is described in the following pages.

Reviewing Collected Information

Before beginning work on Summary Reports, teachers review the information they have collected on each child. This should consist of:

- Developmental Checklist
- Portfolio
- Observation notes
- Information from the child's family
- Information from specialists

This information should be ready for review before teachers begin to complete Summary Reports. Checklist ratings should be finished and Portfolios should be organized before beginning on the Summary Reports. It is important that teachers not try to do all of these tasks at once.

Evaluating and Rating Student Performance and Progress

The Summary Report formalizes and summarizes teachers' evaluations of student performance and student progress in each of the seven Work Sampling domains. Figure 1 shows the rating categories.

FIGURE 1
Explanation of Summary Report rating categories

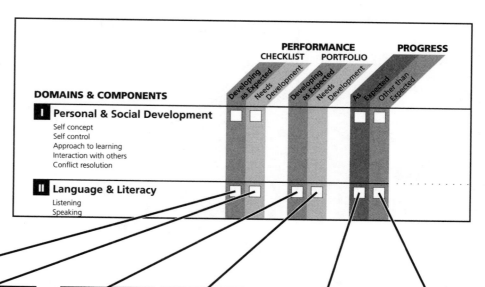

Developing as Expected
The child's current level of performance meets (or exceeds) expectations for this age or grade. Work is in the "Proficient" and "In Process" categories with very few items marked "Not Yet."

Needs Development
The child's current level of performance does not meet expectations for this age or grade. The child's work is primarily in the "Not Yet" category with some "In Process" and very few "Proficient" ratings.

Developing as Expected
Core and Individualized Items provide evidence of appropriate or greater than expected skills, knowledge, behavior, and accomplishments, as compared to classroom expectations.

Needs Development
Core and Individualized Items provide evidence that the child has not yet developed skills, knowledge, or behaviors expected for this classroom.

As Expected
Growth and development in skills, behavior, and knowledge since entering the classroom are appropriate for this child.

Other than Expected
Growth and development in skills, behavior, and knowledge since entering the classroom are either below or above expectations for this child.

After gathering and reviewing all relevant information about a student, the teacher evaluates and rates the child's:

- Performance, based on the Developmental Checklist

- Performance, as displayed in the Portfolio

- Progress

These three rating tasks are described in the next three sections.

EVALUATION OF PERFORMANCE BASED ON THE DEVELOPMENTAL CHECKLIST

The first task faced by the teacher is determining the student's performance rating according to information from the Developmental Checklist. The teacher reflects upon each child and evaluates each child's performance against the standards or expectations for all children at that grade level as identified in the Developmental Guidelines.

The teacher begins by reviewing the ratings s/he made on the Checklist indicators. Within each domain, s/he must determine whether a child's performance is *"Developing as Expected"* or *"Needs Development."* "Developing as Expected" signifies that the child's performance meets or exceeds expectations as identified in the Developmental Guidelines for children at this grade level. "Needs Development" means that the child's performance does not meet these expectations.

To summarize the Checklist ratings, the teacher begins by examining the pattern of ratings within each domain. When most of the child's ratings are in the "Proficient" and "In Process" categories, with only a few items marked "Not Yet," performance is rated as "Developing as Expected" (Figure 2).

FIGURE 2
"Developing as Expected"

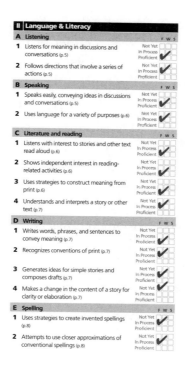

However, when the majority of the ratings fall in the "Not Yet" category, with some "In Process," and very few "Proficient," performance is evaluated as "Needs Development" (Figure 3).

FIGURE 3
"Needs Development"

In most instances, this approach to evaluation provides a good estimate of performance on the Checklist. However, some children's ratings may be evenly distributed across the three checklist-rating categories, or all ratings may be "In Process." In either of these cases, the teacher must take into account two other factors: her/his level of concern about the child's performance, and the time of the school year.

Consider the next example (Figure 4). A child showing this pattern of ratings is evaluated as "Developing as Expected" on the Summary Report in the fall because the teacher knows that the child had difficulty adjusting to the new classroom. However, when this pattern persists after the winter collection period, the teacher decides to evaluate the child's performance as "Needs Development." The child has now adjusted to the new classroom and teacher, and has had many opportunities to develop new skills and behaviors. However, s/he has mastered very few skills, and as a result the teacher decides that the child's performance in this domain "Needs Development."

FIGURE 4
"Developing as Expected" in the fall, but if pattern persists into winter, the rating changes to "Needs Development"

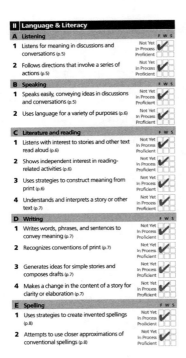

EVALUATION OF PERFORMANCE DISPLAYED IN THE PORTFOLIO Evaluating performance as shown in the Portfolio requires a different approach from evaluating performance on the Checklist because the standard for comparison differs. In many classrooms, each student's Portfolio will be different, reflecting the unique interests, accomplishments, and work styles of the students. Because of this diversity, the teacher must review the learning opportunities s/he has provided for students and formulate reasonable expectations for student work. Then s/he considers whether each student's work meets these expectations.

Performance on the Portfolio is also rated using the categories "Developing as Expected" or "Needs Development." Once again, "Developing as Expected" means that the child's performance, as demonstrated in the Portfolio, meets or exceeds the expectations described below. A rating of "Needs Development" indicates that the child's work does not meet the teacher's expectations.

Teachers' expectations for student work guide their ratings of performance of Portfolio work. Teacher expectations arise from three sources:

1   Teachers may refer to the Guidelines as well as other sources of information about child development for descriptions of what children of different ages are able to do and how they represent their learning.

2   Through professional experience, teachers learn how children of different ages respond to the tasks and learning opportunities presented.

3   By means of the ongoing process of reviewing and selecting work for student Portfolios, teachers develop a store of knowledge concerning how students respond to classroom activities. When teachers evaluate a student's Portfolio work, they base the evaluation on their knowledge of how all the students in the classroom responded to similar learning activities.

Teachers evaluate student performance by considering how well each student's work meets expectations for students of this age or grade, at this time of year, given the opportunities they have provided.

When it is time to evaluate Portfolios for the Summary Report ratings, the teacher selects a domain to evaluate first. Consider the following example of a teacher rating Mathematical Thinking as demonstrated in the Portfolio for the winter collection period: After finding the Mathematical Thinking Core Item folder and the Individualized Item folder s/he reviews the Portfolio Item Record Post-it notes on the Core and Individualized Items that provide information about student performance in Mathematical Thinking. Next, s/he reviews the actual Core Items and Individualized Items that document Mathematical Thinking. Finally, s/he assigns an evaluation rating of the student's performance in Mathematical Thinking for the winter collection period. When evaluating Core Items, the teacher evaluates only the area of learning that the work has been selected to represent. At this time she ignores other characteristics such as neatness, fine motor control, language facility, or artistic features.

EVALUATION OF PROGRESS   Within each domain, teachers are asked to evaluate whether a student's progress is *"As Expected"* or *"Other than Expected."* They use the Checklist ratings and the Portfolio work as evidence for the progress rating. To make this decision, teachers compare a student's performance across collection periods. In other words, the child's current performance is compared with his/her earlier performance. Because children in many early childhood classrooms show as much as a two year developmental span, having previously established standards for rating progress is not possible. Therefore, teachers use their knowledge of child development and teaching experience as guides when they consider whether a child has shown sufficient growth since the previous evaluation and determine the progress rating.

The "Other than Expected" rating is used whenever a child's progress is not typical. Therefore, a child who displays progress beyond expectations, as well as a child who shows less progress than expected, will be rated as "Other than Expected." The teacher adds comments to the report to describe the amount or lack of progress reflected by the rating.

For example, for the winter Summary Report, the teacher reviews the winter Checklist ratings and compares them with the fall Checklist ratings. She also reviews Portfolio work from the winter and compares it with the fall work samples. If the child has made appropriate growth, then the child's progress is rated "As Expected." If, instead, the child's performance as indicated by checklist ratings and work samples has not changed since the previous collection period, or has shown exceptional growth beyond expectations, then the child's progress is rated as "Other than Expected." Any time teachers rate a child's progress as "Other than Expected" they should explain the reasons for this rating in the commentary section of the Summary Report.

After completing the performance and progress ratings for each domain, it is time to begin planning the commentary.

Writing the Commentary

The commentary explains the performance and progress ratings, and emphasizes important and unique aspects of each student. As teachers plan their commentaries, they make decisions about organization, content, and language.

COMMENTARY ORGANIZATION Teachers can use several approaches to structure and organize their comments. These approaches include: 1) writing a paragraph for each domain, 2) writing an integrated report that allots different amounts of space for each domain, or 3) identifying the most important information about the child and writing comments about those major points only.

1 **Domain paragraphs.** Many teachers write a paragraph for each domain that highlights the child's strengths and areas of difficulty, and

includes instructional plans. The teacher incorporates performance and progress information into each paragraph.

2 Integrated reports. Teachers who feel constrained by writing only one paragraph per domain can write an integrated report about the child. It would cover each domain, but some domains would have more detail than others. This method permits teachers to allot space according to the importance of each domain to each child's learning.

3 Highlight reports. Some teachers select several major points about the child that are most important to communicate to the family. They then write comments constructed around these points.

Individual teachers make choices about the organization they will use, as well as deciding whether to write sentences or phrases. Although the commentary section is divided into domains with faint lines, the teacher can decide how much space to allot for each domain.

COMMENTARY CONTENT This section addresses such content-related issues as how much to write and what to write.

How much to write. Teachers often wonder whether they have to write about every component and every indicator for each child. This is not necessary, nor is it recommended. One of the main goals of the Summary Report is to summarize information about a child. Therefore, it is more effective when teachers do not describe all that they know about a child, but integrate, condense, and summarize their knowledge into a form that is understandable to families — in an amount that does not overwhelm them. Although the teacher may not comment on every indicator, or even each component, every domain should be addressed. Consider the following examples from the domain of Personal and Social Development:

EXAMPLE 1
Personal and Social Development

EXAMPLE 2
Personal and Social Development

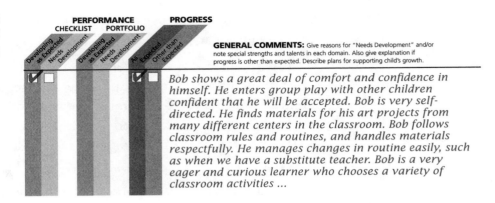

EXAMPLE 3
Personal and Social
Development

GENERAL COMMENTS: Give reasons for "Needs Development" and/or note special strengths and talents in each domain. Also give explanation if progress is other than expected. Describe plans for supporting child's growth.

Bob shows a great deal of comfort and confidence in himself. He enters group play with other children confident that he will be accepted. Bob is very self-directed. He finds materials for his art projects from many different centers in the classroom. Bob follows classroom rules and routines, and handles materials respectfully. He manages changes in routine easily, such as when we have a substitute teacher. Bob is a very eager and curious learner who chooses a variety of classroom activities ...

How much to write is influenced by the type of information the teacher wants the family to have. The brevity of Example 1 is permissible, given the positive tone of the message. In the case of Example 2, the nature of the message warrants a lengthier response. When a child is having difficulty in a particular domain, the teacher should write longer, more detailed, and descriptive comments. Example 2 does not communicate how Terry becomes involved in conflicts or how the teacher is going to help him learn to interact more cooperatively with peers. Negative comments require support; otherwise they are not very useful. Having specific details and examples will be helpful to the teacher and family members during the conference. It is unnecessary and overly time-consuming to address every indicator, as in Example 3, for a child who is succeeding in a domain. However, being clear and providing specifics is always beneficial.

What to write. The goal of the commentary section of the Summary Report is to provide a profile of an individual student's strengths and areas of concern across the seven domains. These comments allow teachers to highlight the unique learning characteristics, interests, and accomplishments of each child. The quality of the student's work, as well as the child's level of performance, should be addressed. When domains are rated as "Needs Development," the teacher has an opportunity to elaborate on the rating by providing specific information about learning goals. In the winter and at the end of the year, the teacher should also comment on student progress, especially if that progress is rated "Other than Expected."

Addressing strengths and areas of concern. Teachers who structure their comments by domain may want to organize their comments according to the components. By addressing components that represent strengths before commenting on the components that are problematic, teachers can convey a positive tone that emphasizes the child's current level of competence.

EXAMPLE 4
Personal and Social
Development

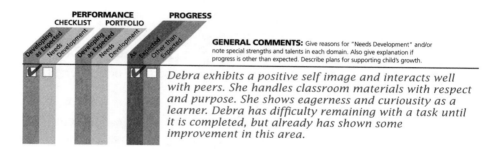

GENERAL COMMENTS: Give reasons for "Needs Development" and/or note special strengths and talents in each domain. Also give explanation if progress is other than expected. Describe plans for supporting child's growth.

Debra exhibits a positive self image and interacts well with peers. She handles classroom materials with respect and purpose. She shows eagerness and curiousity as a learner. Debra has difficulty remaining with a task until it is completed, but already has shown some improvement in this area.

EXAMPLE 5
Mathematical Thinking

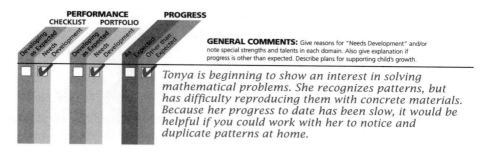

GENERAL COMMENTS: Give reasons for "Needs Development" and/or note special strengths and talents in each domain. Also give explanation if progress is other than expected. Describe plans for supporting child's growth.

Tonya is beginning to show an interest in solving mathematical problems. She recognizes patterns, but has difficulty reproducing them with concrete materials. Because her progress to date has been slow, it would be helpful if you could work with her to notice and duplicate patterns at home.

EXAMPLE 6
Mathematical Thinking

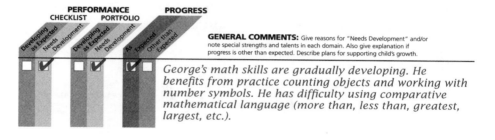

GENERAL COMMENTS: Give reasons for "Needs Development" and/or note special strengths and talents in each domain. Also give explanation if progress is other than expected. Describe plans for supporting child's growth.

George's math skills are gradually developing. He benefits from practice counting objects and working with number symbols. He has difficulty using comparative mathematical language (more than, less than, greatest, largest, etc.).

EXAMPLE 7
Language and Literacy

GENERAL COMMENTS: Give reasons for "Needs Development" and/or note special strengths and talents in each domain. Also give explanation if progress is other than expected. Describe plans for supporting child's growth.

Tyrell follows 2-to-3 step directions and speaks clearly when conveying his ideas and thoughts. He listens with interest to stories read aloud and can tell or draw events very well. He is gradually gaining confidence as a writer and uses invented spelling to write simple sentences, although this is only beginning to be reflected in his Portfolio.

Explaining the ratings. Another function of the commentary on the Summary Report is to explain performance and progress ratings. In particular, when the ratings appear to conflict, the Summary Report allows teachers to describe and explain these apparent discrepancies. In this way, the commentary supports the ratings, but it also provides greater clarity about individual students than the ratings.

Several combinations of ratings may elicit confusion or questions from the student's family. Within a domain, the Checklist and Portfolio ratings may differ, or the Performance and Progress ratings may differ. At first glance, these combinations may not make sense. However these combinations can be valid, accurately reflecting the child's learning and performance in the classroom. Further explanation of this is provided later in this chapter, in the section entitled "Frequently Asked Questions."

COMMENTARY LANGUAGE The writing on the Summary Report should support its major goal: to communicate constructive and clear information about child performance and progress in easily understood language. Comments should be specific, include examples, and avoid the use of educational jargon. The report should be positive in tone and respect the child's efforts and achievements.

Be specific and descriptive. Comments are most meaningful to families when they are specific and descriptive, rather than abstract and vague. Below are three descriptions of a kindergartner's Personal and Social Development. Consider which example provides a sense of the individual child. Which gives the most descriptive information? If you were the parent of a kindergarten-age child, which of these comments would you most like to receive?

EXAMPLE 8
Personal and Social
Development

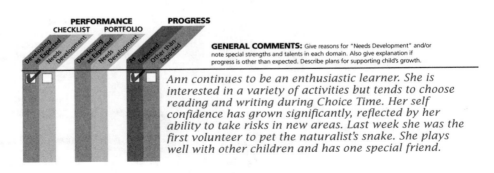

GENERAL COMMENTS: Give reasons for "Needs Development" and/or note special strengths and talents in each domain. Also give explanation if progress is other than expected. Describe plans for supporting child's growth.

Ann continues to be an enthusiastic learner. She is interested in a variety of activities but tends to choose reading and writing during Choice Time. Her self confidence has grown significantly, reflected by her ability to take risks in new areas. Last week she was the first volunteer to pet the naturalist's snake. She plays well with other children and has one special friend.

EXAMPLE 9
Personal and Social
Development

GENERAL COMMENTS: Give reasons for "Needs Development" and/or note special strengths and talents in each domain. Also give explanation if progress is other than expected. Describe plans for supporting child's growth.

Candy enjoys selecting a variety of Choice Time activities. She works and plays alongside others and is beginning to interact more easily with children and adults in large group situations.

EXAMPLE 10
Personal and Social
Development

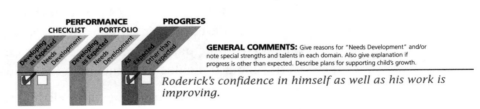

GENERAL COMMENTS: Give reasons for "Needs Development" and/or note special strengths and talents in each domain. Also give explanation if progress is other than expected. Describe plans for supporting child's growth.

Roderick's confidence in himself as well as his work is improving.

Example 8 provides both general and specific information. The reader can see that Ann's teacher knows her quite well. Examples 9 and 10 give very general information, and do not provide an individualized picture of how these two children learn and work.

Use language directly from the Developmental Guidelines. Teachers may find it helpful to use language from the Guidelines, as Glen's teacher does (Example 11). If teachers incorporate language from the Guidelines, it is important that they add specific examples unique to the child, so that the report retains a sense of the child's individuality.

EXAMPLE 11
Language and Literacy

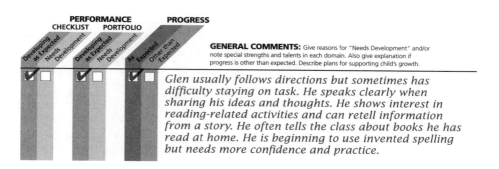

PERFORMANCE   **PROGRESS**
CHECKLIST   **PORTFOLIO**

GENERAL COMMENTS: Give reasons for "Needs Development" and/or note special strengths and talents in each domain. Also give explanation if progress is other than expected. Describe plans for supporting child's growth.

Glen usually follows directions but sometimes has difficulty staying on task. He speaks clearly when sharing his ideas and thoughts. He shows interest in reading-related activities and can retell information from a story. He often tells the class about books he has read at home. He is beginning to use invented spelling but needs more confidence and practice.

Individualize the commentary. Note how this first-grade teacher described Trey's performance in Scientific Thinking:

EXAMPLE 12
Scientific Thinking

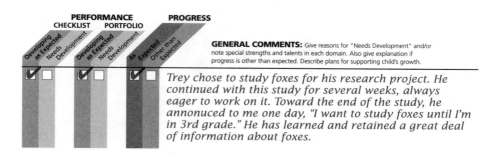

PERFORMANCE   **PROGRESS**
CHECKLIST   **PORTFOLIO**

GENERAL COMMENTS: Give reasons for "Needs Development" and/or note special strengths and talents in each domain. Also give explanation if progress is other than expected. Describe plans for supporting child's growth.

Trey chose to study foxes for his research project. He continued with this study for several weeks, always eager to work on it. Toward the end of the study, he announced to me one day, "I want to study foxes until I'm in 3rd grade." He has learned and retained a great deal of information about foxes.

Using the child's own words personalizes this comment in a striking way.

Be positive. The writing on the Summary Report should be positive. It is best to begin and end the report with a positive comment. Moreover, the report should state what a child can do, not only what s/he is unable to do. It may be helpful to discuss with colleagues how to say what children are not yet capable of doing in positive ways without being misleading about the level of the child's performance. Examples 13 and 14 show how a negative comment can be changed into a more positive statement.

EXAMPLE 13
Personal and Social
Development

GENERAL COMMENTS: Give reasons for "Needs Development" and/or note special strengths and talents in each domain. Also give explanation if progress is other than expected. Describe plans for supporting child's growth.

Because Steven is a very quiet child, it is hard to determine his thoughts. He interacts well with others and is respectful of their belongings. However, he doesn't show any eagerness to learn, lacks participation within a group, and daydreams instead of seeking help.

EXAMPLE 14
Personal and Social
Development

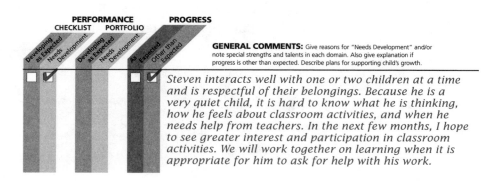

GENERAL COMMENTS: Give reasons for "Needs Development" and/or note special strengths and talents in each domain. Also give explanation if progress is other than expected. Describe plans for supporting child's growth.

Steven interacts well with one or two children at a time and is respectful of their belongings. Because he is a very quiet child, it is hard to know what he is thinking, how he feels about classroom activities, and when he needs help from teachers. In the next few months, I hope to see greater interest and participation in classroom activities. We will work together on learning when it is appropriate for him to ask for help with his work.

Below is another example of a comment with a negative tone. Think about how to state it more positively. Remember that it is best to begin and end with a positive comment.

EXAMPLE 15
Personal and Social
Development

GENERAL COMMENTS: Give reasons for "Needs Development" and/or note special strengths and talents in each domain. Also give explanation if progress is other than expected. Describe plans for supporting child's growth.

Courtney has shown little growth in this domain. She rarely makes independent decisions or assumes independent responsibility for completing her work. She has difficulty following class rules. Courtney has many friends, but needs to learn to interact more comfortably with adults.

For students who are struggling in specific areas, it is helpful to state first what the child can do, and then discuss the skills you will be concentrating on improving in the future (Examples 16, 17, and 18). Another approach is to comment on current capabilities and then set goals or project the skills you hope the child will attain by the end of the year (Examples 19 and 20).

EXAMPLE 16
Mathematical Thinking

GENERAL COMMENTS: Give reasons for "Needs Development" and/or note special strengths and talents in each domain. Also give explanation if progress is other than expected. Describe plans for supporting child's growth.

Sally has mastered addition of two-digit numbers. During the next few weeks, we will be focusing on subtraction.

EXAMPLE 17
Language and Literacy

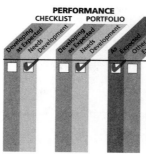

GENERAL COMMENTS: Give reasons for "Needs Development" and/or note special strengths and talents in each domain. Also give explanation if progress is other than expected. Describe plans for supporting child's growth.

Ted's interest in language and reading can be seen by his eagerness to listen to stories read aloud and willingness to draw pictures in his journal. He is not yet writing words to accompany his pictures and seems reluctant to speak up during class discussions. In the next few months, I will focus attention on and support his growth in these areas.

EXAMPLE 18
Personal and Social
Development

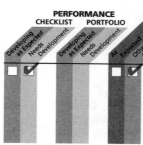

GENERAL COMMENTS: Give reasons for "Needs Development" and/or note special strengths and talents in each domain. Also give explanation if progress is other than expected. Describe plans for supporting child's growth.

Although Jerome continues to make progress in all academic areas, his overall attitude has not been as positive this past marking period. He seems more impatient with others and is easily frustrated. He's working on solving conflicts appropriately and also on getting assignments done in a reasonable period of time.

EXAMPLE 19
Mathematical Thinking

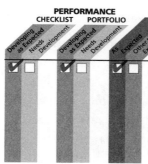

GENERAL COMMENTS: Give reasons for "Needs Development" and/or note special strengths and talents in each domain. Also give explanation if progress is other than expected. Describe plans for supporting child's growth.

Pat's free exploration of manipulatives reflects her enjoyment of math as well as good readiness skills. She recognizes, extends, and creates patterns, understands the concept of number and quantity (0–10), instantly recognizes the number of dots on a die (1–6), and has a beginning sense of geometry, measurement, graphing, and math vocabulary. A goal is to develop her number operation in adding two quantitities.

EXAMPLE 20
Personal and Social
Development

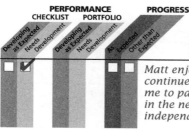

GENERAL COMMENTS: Give reasons for "Needs Development" and/or note special strengths and talents in each domain. Also give explanation if progress is other than expected. Describe plans for supporting child's growth.

Matt enjoys coming to the morning meeting. He continues to need individual guidance and support from me to pariticpate in group discussions. My goal for Matt in the next few months is for him to develop greater independence in this area.

When teachers pay close attention to the tone of their comments, families can read Summary Reports and feel hopeful and confident about their child's development. Summary Reports should never convey a primitive tone.

Now, take a moment to compare Examples 21 and 22. Which is more positive?

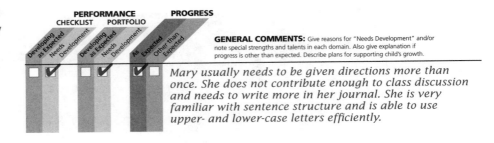

Mary usually needs to be given directions more than once. She does not contribute enough to class discussion and needs to write more in her journal. She is very familiar with sentence structure and is able to use upper- and lower-case letters efficiently.

EXAMPLE 22
Language and Literacy

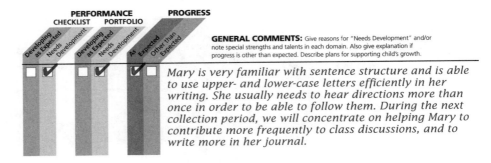

Mary is very familiar with sentence structure and is able to use upper- and lower-case letters efficiently in her writing. She usually needs to hear directions more than once in order to be able to follow them. During the next collection period, we will concentrate on helping Mary to contribute more frequently to class discussions, and to write more in her journal.

A comment takes on a more positive tone when teachers state what the child can do before presenting areas of concern.

Be respectful. The final point about the language on the Summary Report is that it should demonstrate respect for children, their approaches to learning, and accomplishments. Teachers should be careful about word choice and avoid the use of colloquialisms or slang that may be misinterpreted. In Example 23, the teacher uses very strong, provocative language that may be interpreted differently by different readers ("bossy, sulky, and stubborn"). Example 24 shows how this comment could be rewritten.

EXAMPLE 23
Personal and Social
Development

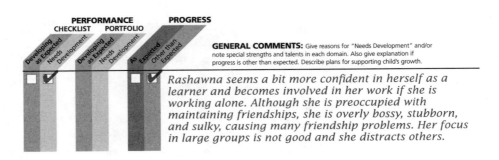

Rashawna seems a bit more confident in herself as a learner and becomes involved in her work if she is working alone. Although she is preoccupied with maintaining friendships, she is overly bossy, stubborn, and sulky, causing many friendship problems. Her focus in large groups is not good and she distracts others.

EXAMPLE 24
Personal and Social
Development

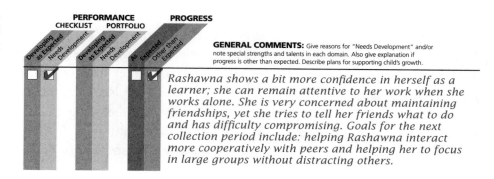

GENERAL COMMENTS: Give reasons for "Needs Development" and/or note special strengths and talents in each domain. Also give explanation if progress is other than expected. Describe plans for supporting child's growth.

Rashawna shows a bit more confidence in herself as a learner; she can remain attentive to her work when she works alone. She is very concerned about maintaining friendships, yet she tries to tell her friends what to do and has difficulty compromising. Goals for the next collection period include: helping Rashawna interact more cooperatively with peers and helping her to focus in large groups without distracting others.

Sharing the Summary Report with Families

The Summary Report should be discussed with families at a conference, rather than sent home without personal contact. Some teachers send the Summary Report home and then ask parents to bring it with them to the conference. This allows the family time to read the report and to formulate questions privately before coming in for the conference. Family members with limited reading skills will need the report read to them during the family-teacher conference.

Some teachers have found it helpful to describe their classroom curriculum in a statement attached to each Summary Report (see Appendix C). This is especially important if a conference will not be held.

Frequently Asked Questions about the Summary Report

As teachers complete Summary Reports, especially during the first year of implementation, the following questions often arise:

Q *When should I start completing Summary Reports?*

A About two to three weeks before the end of the collection period or before parent conferences begin, you should start to work on Summary Reports. It is very important that the Checklist ratings have already been completed and that the Portfolios are in order.

Q *I'm ready to start completing Summary Reports. I'm surrounded by piles of Checklists, Portfolios, observational notes, and other materials. What should I do first?*

A Teachers organize their work on Summary Reports in several different ways. Some teachers begin by making Checklist ratings or Portfolio ratings for every student in their class in every domain. Other teachers gather all the information they have on a particular child and complete that child's entire Summary Report. Still other teachers evaluate the entire class for one domain before going on to the next domain, for example, evaluating every child's Personal and Social Development before evaluating Language and Literacy.

Regardless of method, the process begins with a review of documentation and evidence. For example, if you decide to organize your work by domain, you might start with Language and Literacy. Then, begin by reviewing the Checklist in the Language and Literacy Domain, and make a determination about performance. (This is one of the reasons that it is so important to complete students' Checklists before beginning Summary Reports.) Next, you would review the Core and Individualized Items in the Portfolio and rate performance as demonstrated in the Portfolio. Finally, review all available information from the Checklists and Portfolios and rate the child's progress from the beginning of the school year.

Q *How does performance differ from progress?*

A Performance and progress have two very different meanings. *Performance* refers to the level of a student's behavior, skills, and accomplishments at a particular point in time. In the Work Sampling System, the student's current level of performance is documented in two ways: by the teacher's observations as recorded on the Checklist and by the child's work as represented in the Portfolio. Performance is evaluated on the Summary Report near the end of each collection period. The ratings describe whether the child's performance within a particular domain is "Developing as Expected" or "Needs Development" as compared with expectations for children in a particular grade.

In contrast, the *progress* rating focuses on growth or change over time. The child's current performance is compared with his/her previous performance. The progress rating does not involve comparing this particular student's progress with an external measure of progress. Instead, progress is evaluated within the context of each child's work; the child is only compared with him/herself. You are asked to determine whether the child's progress within each domain is "As Expected" or "Other than Expected" as compared with prior performance. Rapid or exceptional progress as well as slow progress should be noted in this column and accompanied by explanatory comments in the narrative.

Q *Should I evaluate progress in the fall?*

A At the end of the fall collection period, the progress rating is optional. Sometimes, however, teachers have observed enough growth from the beginning of school to the end of the fall collection period that they feel comfortable making a progress rating. This decision is left to the individual teacher and may vary from child to child within a classroom.

Q *Should performance and progress ratings always agree?*

A Performance and progress ratings are not always the same. Children may perform as we expect them to and still not show growth. Or the opposite may be true. For example, the performance of a student with special needs may be delayed in several domains. However, this child may also show excellent progress when his current performance is compared with his previous performance within a particular domain (Examples 25 and 26). Similarly, a second grader who is unable to identify letters in September but who is sounding out words in March, may be rated as "Needs Development" for performance on the Checklist and Portfolio in Language and Literacy, but his/her progress is rated "As Expected." These different ratings make sense when the performance standards for each component of the Work Sampling System and the standard for progress are kept in mind.

EXAMPLE 25
Language and Literacy

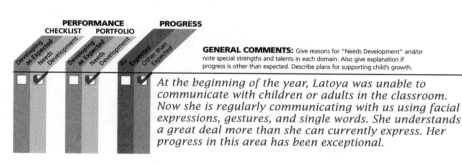

GENERAL COMMENTS: Give reasons for "Needs Development" and/or note special strengths and talents in each domain. Also give explanation if progress is other than expected. Describe plans for supporting child's growth.

At the beginning of the year, Latoya was unable to communicate with children or adults in the classroom. Now she is regularly communicating with us using facial expressions, gestures, and single words. She understands a great deal more than she can currently express. Her progress in this area has been exceptional.

EXAMPLE 26
Language and Literacy

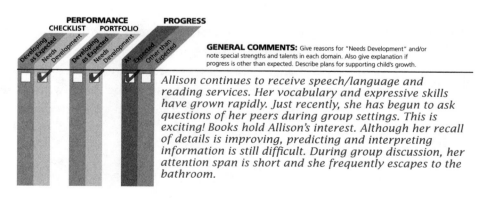

GENERAL COMMENTS: Give reasons for "Needs Development" and/or note special strengths and talents in each domain. Also give explanation if progress is other than expected. Describe plans for supporting child's growth.

Allison continues to receive speech/language and reading services. Her vocabulary and expressive skills have grown rapidly. Just recently, she has begun to ask questions of her peers during group settings. This is exciting! Books hold Allison's interest. Although her recall of details is improving, predicting and interpreting information is still difficult. During group discussion, her attention span is short and she frequently escapes to the bathroom.

Q *Should performance ratings be the same for the Checklist and Portfolio?*

A Not necessarily. Sometimes a student's performance is rated as "Developing as Expected" on the Checklist and as "Needs Development" on the Portfolio. In this case, a teacher's observations and Checklist ratings show that a student's accomplishments and skills in Mathematical Thinking are "Developing as Expected" when compared with national expectations. However, the student's work in the Portfolio did not meet the teacher's standards. One reason for this combination of ratings concerns the difference in scope of the Checklist and the Portfolio. It may be that the student has difficulty understanding the areas of learning sampled by the Core Items of the Portfolio.

For example, a child may be quite competent overall in Mathematical Thinking. However, s/he is confused by standard measurement and does not understand many concepts related to Probability and Statistics. If these are the two areas of learning selected as the basis for Core Items, the child's Portfolio performance rating might be "Needs Development," while the Checklist rating for Mathematical Thinking might be "Developing as Expected." In this case, the teacher might write the following:

EXAMPLE 27
Mathematical Thinking

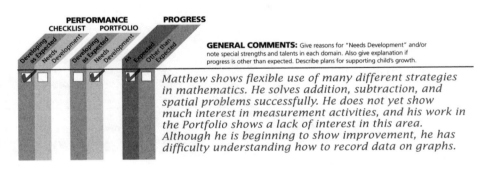

GENERAL COMMENTS: Give reasons for "Needs Development" and/or note special strengths and talents in each domain. Also give explanation if progress is other than expected. Describe plans for supporting child's growth.

Matthew shows flexible use of many different strategies in mathematics. He solves addition, subtraction, and spatial problems successfully. He does not yet show much interest in measurement activities, and his work in the Portfolio shows a lack of interest in this area. Although he is beginning to show improvement, he has difficulty understanding how to record data on graphs.

Another reason for a discrepancy between Checklist and Portfolio performance ratings within a domain may be a child's inability to sustain attention in order to complete work. For example, a child may not be able to complete written book reports, but shows mastery of comprehension of story structure, plot, and character when allowed to demonstrate his/her knowledge verbally. However, the child is unable to demonstrate this knowledge in the Portfolio because of difficulty in sustaining attention to written work (Examples 28 and 29).

EXAMPLE 28
Scientific Thinking

GENERAL COMMENTS: Give reasons for "Needs Development" and/or note special strengths and talents in each domain. Also give explanation if progress is other than expected. Describe plans for supporting child's growth.

Isaiah is very observant and interested in the natural world. But he is not able to relay this to others because of his difficulty in expressing his thoughts in writing and his hesitancy to participate in discussions.

EXAMPLE 29
Language and Literacy

GENERAL COMMENTS: Give reasons for "Needs Development" and/or note special strengths and talents in each domain. Also give explanation if progress is other than expected. Describe plans for supporting child's growth.

Maria loves listening to stories and follows complicated plots with relative ease. However, she is unable to express her understanding in writing or drawing. During the next few months, we will audiotape Maria as she retells stories she has heard and try to extend her verbal skills into written work as she listens to her own words.

A different example is given by a child who is rated as "Developing as Expected" for the Portfolio and as "Needs Development" for the Check-list. Within the domain of Mathematical Thinking, the specified areas of learning may be Geometry and Spatial Relations and Patterns and Relationships. The child may be doing excellent work in these two areas, but may have difficulty understanding number concepts and operations, probability and statistics, and measurement. In this case, the Checklist performance rating would be "Needs Development." However, the Portfolio work may show that the child is developing as expected in Geometry and Spatial Relations and Patterns and Relationships.

EXAMPLE 30
Mathematical Thinking

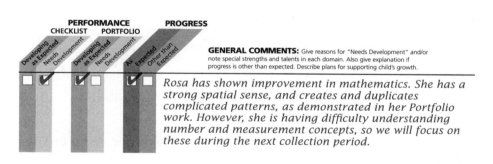

GENERAL COMMENTS: Give reasons for "Needs Development" and/or note special strengths and talents in each domain. Also give explanation if progress is other than expected. Describe plans for supporting child's growth.

Rosa has shown improvement in mathematics. She has a strong spatial sense, and creates and duplicates complicated patterns, as demonstrated in her Portfolio work. However, she is having difficulty understanding number and measurement concepts, so we will focus on these during the next collection period.

Q *Why is it necessary to make a judgment, rather than just describe a child's current performance?*

A Some teachers feel that having external standards and evaluating students according to those standards may not be equitable. Because all children do not start school with the same advantages, it may seem unfair to evaluate them with the same yardstick. With Work Sampling, children are evaluated against several different standards:

■ The Developmental Guidelines and Checklists describe reasonable expectations for children at different grade levels based on *state and national standards.*

■ Portfolio work is evaluated within the context of *local (classroom and school) standards.*

■ Children's progress is evaluated in terms of the *individual child.*

Having standards for learning ensures that we regularly take stock of children's performance and progress, so that we may better adapt our teaching to their needs.

It is important to acknowledge that teachers make informal evaluative decisions on a daily basis. As teachers observe students in the classroom, they evaluate students' interactions with activities, and develop and adjust their instructional plans. When teachers review work samples for inclusion in the Portfolio, they internally monitor whether the work meets their expectations, expectations that are set both by interacting with other professionals and through numerous "portfolio conferences" held with students. These daily assessment decisions help to create subsequent learning plans.

When you engage in the process of completing the Summary Reports, you make similar evaluative decisions, but in a more formalized way. The Summary Report allows you to summarize your knowledge of the student's work and behavior over a longer period of time. Evaluative decisions are based on the accumulated evidence from many sources of information gathered during the collection period.

Q *How do you know you are maintaining standards?*

A Work Sampling's Developmental Guidelines and Checklists are based on state and national standards for curriculum. It is essential that teachers follow the Guidelines and apply them when making evaluations. Portfolios do not have similar national standards, but instead emerge from the teacher's own classroom or community. By regularly observing students and reviewing Portfolio contents with students and colleagues, you clarify your own standards of assessment and transmit these standards to your students.

Q *How do I know I am making objective and fair decisions?*

A Because the ratings and comments on the Summary Report are based on extensive evidence and documentation of the child's work and behavior collected over time, you are less likely to be influenced by whether the student was having a good or bad day on the day you write the report. Similarly, your stress level, or the performance of the student whose report you have most recently completed should not influence your evaluation because of the extensive evidence accumulated on each student's performance. The process of evaluation requires that you step back, review your knowledge of each child (supported by observations, Checklist ratings, and work in the Portfolio), and reflect on the overall picture before synthesizing these sources of information into a portrait of the child. Bias has no place in assessment, and the information described above is intended to neutralize its potential impact.

Q *Why include comments?*

A Comments are included for several important reasons. First, teacher comments describe and explain the performance and progress ratings. Although two children may have identical ratings, it is unlikely that these two children have acquired the same skills and knowledge. For example, two first grade children may be "Developing as Expected" in Mathematical Thinking. However, one of them is very strong in creating patterns and understanding spatial relationships but has difficulty with simple addition and subtraction. Another student understands number concepts and operations and performs computations accurately, but has great difficulty perceiving patterns and understanding the relationship between shapes. The commentary allows you to explain and describe each child's performance in a more specific and detailed way.

The second reason for including comments on the Summary Report is to individualize and personalize the report. Although two children may have fairly similar skills, it is unlikely that they will demonstrate their skills and knowledge in the same fashion. For example, three third graders, all rated as "Developing as Expected" in Language and Literacy, may use strategies to extract meaning from print equally well. However, one child reads voraciously and uses books to find information about topics of personal interest, another reads for pleasure and escape, and the third reads efficiently but finds enjoyment in writing fantasy stories. The commentary allows you to describe not only skills the child has acquired, but also how the child demonstrates those skills. Just as student work in the Portfolio elaborates what can be learned from the Checklist ratings, the commentary on the Summary Report enriches the information provided by the performance and progress ratings.

Q *How long does it take to complete a Summary Report?*

A Because teachers have different ways of working, it is difficult to answer this question simply. A teacher who rapidly finds a comfortable way to gather and review Checklists and Portfolios, and who writes with ease will require much less time per student to complete a Summary Report than a teacher who is overwhelmed with the amount of information and is uncomfortable writing comments. It is important to realize that completing Summary Reports the first time may take twice as long as the second time. The more often you complete Summary Reports the more natural it will be to describe children in these terms.

Q *How should Summary Reports be used at conference time?*

A Work Sampling System conferences rely on the same techniques for establishing rapport and positive working relationships with families as those used with other reporting systems. Work Sampling enriches family-teacher relationships by offering extensive documentation to share with families. Most teachers structure the conference around the Summary Report, and use examples from the Portfolio to illustrate important points. Although the Checklist is primarily designed for use by the teacher, it may be shown to parents to help clarify a student's performance within a particular domain.

Q *How can specialists be involved in Summary Reports?*

A Because expectations for special subject teachers (Art, Music, Physical Education, etc.) vary among districts, each district must decide whether and how special subject teachers will be involved in Work Sampling. This decision will be based in part on the extent of contact that specialists have with students (how frequently they see students and for how long), the specialists' caseloads, and whether specialists had responsibility for student evaluation before the Work Sampling System was adopted. Because of individual policies within school districts, determining the role of specialists in Work Sampling must be addressed on an individual basis, district by district, after consideration of how specialists function and how district and contractual realities constrain the specialist's role. (For further discussion of these issues, see page 121.)

Student evaluation is most accurate and comprehensive when teachers and specialists collaborate. Incorporating a specialist's expertise into a Summary Report enriches the evaluation. Having two views of a child's development within a particular domain provides a more comprehensive, and therefore more reliable, assessment of the child.

The **SPECIAL SUBJECT REPORT** form (Figure 5) has been created for specialists who have independent responsibility for evaluating students, or for those who want to make comments about students. The Special Subject Report form includes four carbonless copies (family, teacher, specialist, school file) and is designed to allow special subject teachers to transmit information to the child's primary teacher and to the child's family. Special subject teachers check the domain(s) that they will address. Some districts require special subject teachers to comment on every student. Others ask teachers to comment only if a child's performance or progress does not meet the teacher's expectations. This is an optional form that may assist special subject teachers in districts where they are responsible for student evaluation.

FIGURE 5
Special Subject Report form

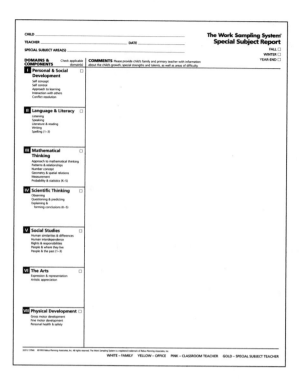

Q *Should Summary Reports be written differently at different times of the year?*

A Although the Summary Report accomplishes the same functions at each collection period, each period's Summary Report also differs slightly in perspective. The fall Summary Report reflects the teacher's initial understanding of the child. Most teachers at this time of the year have a general understanding about what students know in each of the domains, and how students express their knowledge. This first Summary Report provides a baseline measure of the child's skills at the start of the year. Because the child still has many months to acquire the skills and knowledge expected for his/her grade level, and the teacher is only beginning to know the child, ratings made in the fall are often best described as preliminary.

The Summary Report completed at the end of the winter collection period describes what children have learned as well as what they still need to accomplish. By this time, you know the student quite well and are able to use your knowledge to modify instruction to best meet the child's needs. Moreover, with two-thirds of the school year completed, you are fairly confident in your understanding of the child and the ratings you have made.

The year-end report summarizes the child's performance and progress over the course of the year. Here you have the opportunity not only to review the child's performance for the entire school year, but also to discuss progress from the beginning of the year to the end. As teachers become familiar with this method of summarizing a child's learning and reporting to parents, their reports begin to show continuity from one reporting period to another.

Further Discussion about Summary Reports

Issues in Writing the Commentary

Teachers frequently communicate information about students in writing. They send notes home to families, they write questions and thoughts about individual students, and they note observations of students throughout the day. However, the commentary on the Summary Report calls for a different type of writing. Unlike the spontaneous jotting of an anecdotal record, the commentary on the Summary Report is a product of thoughtful reflection based on accumulated evidence from multiple sources.

THE AUDIENCE FOR THE COMMENTARY The audience for the Summary Report influences the kind of information that should be included. The teacher's knowledge of the child's family will help determine the specific content and form of the report. The teacher might consider the following questions.

■ Is the family particularly interested in a specific aspect of the child's learning?

■ Is the child's family familiar with the school's assessment practices?

■ Is a family member highly critical of the child?

■ Is the family distrustful of teachers and schools?

The teacher's writing should take into account what s/he knows about the family and their relationship with the student.

How much contact the teacher has had with the family will also influence the writing of the narrative. The first report to a family who the teacher does not know may be more formal in tone and comprehensive than subsequent reports. A report to a parent who regularly visits the school and volunteers in the classroom may be shorter than reports to parents who are unfamiliar with the classroom, the curriculum, and the scope of activities. If the family frequently communicates with the teacher, the report may reflect the concerns expressed by the family in previous conversations. Whether the Summary Report will be given to the family at a conference will also influence how the report is written.

ADDITIONAL CONTENT FOR THE COMMENTARY As teachers become comfortable writing narrative reports, they may begin to include other types of information including suggestions for the family and descriptions of the child's continuous progress.

Suggestions for the family. Many families want to participate in their child's learning. Suggestions for concrete ways that the family can work with the child at home to further his/her educational goals may also be included in the Summary Report (Example 31). Asking families to help students acquire particular concepts shows that you value their involvement.

EXAMPLE 31
Mathematical Thinking

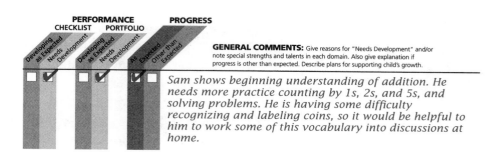

GENERAL COMMENTS: Give reasons for "Needs Development" and/or note special strengths and talents in each domain. Also give explanation if progress is other than expected. Describe plans for supporting child's growth.

Sam shows beginning understanding of addition. He needs more practice counting by 1s, 2s, and 5s, and solving problems. He is having some difficulty recognizing and labeling coins, so it would be helpful to him to work some of this vocabulary into discussions at home.

Continuous progress. Progress is an important focus of the Summary Report. To ensure that the child's current performance is portrayed in the context of the entire school year, it is useful for teachers to review previous reports before beginning to write the current report. It is helpful for parents, especially parents of children who are experiencing difficulties in school, to see that the teacher acknowledges the progress that their child has made. The following comment exemplifies this point:

EXAMPLE 32
Personal and Social
Development

GENERAL COMMENTS: Give reasons for "Needs Development" and/or note special strengths and talents in each domain. Also give explanation if progress is other than expected. Describe plans for supporting child's growth.

After reviewing the fall report, it is clear to me that Susan has moved forward significantly in Personal/Social Development. I do, however, continue to see quite a bit of variation from day to day. At times, Susan is fully involved in whatever is going on; and at other times she stays on the edge of activities watching the other children. However, overall, Susan seems happier and more confident.

Involving Students and Families in Evaluation

The Summary Report and the conference associated with it provide an opportunity for students, families, and teachers to discuss student learning and growth. To maximize its usefulness, the Summary Report should be discussed with the family, rather than sent home without personal contact. In this way, teachers have greater certainty that parents understand the report, and parents will have the opportunity to ask questions, contribute information, and share their concerns.

As much as possible, the student should participate in the Summary Report process. An important reason for and result of student involvement in assessment is the chance to make assessment less mysterious and anxiety-provoking. Rather than viewing assessment as something external to themselves, student involvement transforms assessment into a learning process over which students can feel some control.

The Role of the Student in Evaluation

Work Sampling is very committed to student involvement in the evaluation process. In previous chapters, student roles in the Checklist and Portfolio collection process were described. Similar to the varying levels of student involvement in reviewing and selecting Portfolio items, student involvement with Summary Reports takes many different forms. It is critical that evaluation become a part of the learning process, and that students do not feel that evaluation is a secret, or only of concern to parents and teachers. Steps teachers can take include the following:

1   **Arranging individual meetings with students before family-teacher conferences.** Some teachers have a conference with every student before the family-teacher conference. The teacher reviews the Summary Report with the student and asks him/her if there is any information s/he wants the teacher to communicate to the family.

2   **Asking students to review their work and comment on it.** As the end of a collection period nears, teachers may ask students to review the work they have done during the past 8 to 12 weeks. Students may select particular items that they want the teacher to share with their family. Or they may write a paragraph about their progress and the learning goals they have set for themselves for the next collection period.

3   **Student participation in conferences.** Teachers may invite students to participate in family-teacher conferences. One advantage of this approach is that students do not feel that what happens at the conference is only for adults. By participating in conferences, students are able to see the importance of their education to the teacher and their family.

4   **Student-led conferences.** This represents the highest degree of student participation in the Summary Report and family-teacher conference. It requires advance work by the student and teacher to prepare the student for his/her role in the conference. The teacher and student may discuss the student's work and progress and arrive at a consensus regarding information which is important enough to be shared. Then, the student can select work that illustrates his/her learning.

At the conference, the student introduces his/her family to his/her teacher. Conferences may be scheduled to allow time for the student to give his/her family a tour of the classroom or school. When the conference begins, the student shows his/her work. After the child has had an opportunity to talk about the work, the teacher also adds comments. The conference ends with the teacher, student, and family setting learning goals for the next collection period.

Conclusion

The Summary Report takes the place of traditional report cards. Like report cards, its primary purpose is to communicate information about a child's learning and development to families and other interested parties. However, the Summary Report offers additional benefits. First, it describes the whole child by evaluating performance in the seven Work Sampling domains. Second, it provides a profile of the child's strengths and areas of difficulty across those domains. Children who have difficulty with academic areas can be acknowledged for their particular strengths in The Arts or Physical Development. Third, it focuses on individuals by providing comments and specific examples in addition to ratings of performance and progress. Finally, by recognizing progress and identifying plans to support children's learning, it validates and supports children's efforts as they grow in competence and accomplishment.

CHAPTER 5

Special Topics

THIS CHAPTER ADDRESSES A VARIETY OF TOPICS THAT ARISE AS TEACHers begin to learn about and implement the Work Sampling System. It includes discussions of:

- Using the Work Sampling System in Preschool Classrooms
- Assessing Children with Special Needs
- Involving Special Subject Teachers
- Using Work Sampling in Multi-Age Classrooms
- Informing the Community about the Work Sampling System

Using Work Sampling in Preschool Classrooms

The Work Sampling System was originally developed as an assessment for kindergarten and preschool children. The earliest version consisted of a developmental checklist and emphasized the importance of teacher observation in the assessment process. The extension of Work Sampling to the elementary grades highlighted the connections between preschool experiences and the academic learning of later years, and helped teachers recognize how preschool education creates a foundation for later cognitive and academic learning. In this way, the Work Sampling System validates the curriculum of the early years.

The use of the Work Sampling System in preschool classrooms differs from its use in elementary classrooms in two important ways. First, the Portfolio Collection Process requires greater involvement of the teacher. Because the work of preschool children centers on process and exploration, and because preschoolers do not create many products on their own, their teachers must assume greater responsibility for documenting and representing children's learning processes in order to preserve them in a Portfolio.

Second, the actual implementation of the Work Sampling System in preschool classrooms may vary from implementation at the elementary level. These differences are necessary because preschool (and many kindergarten) programs frequently have shorter or fewer school days than elementary schools. Children may attend for half days, or attend only two to four days per week. Some preschools start later in the fall than elementary programs and often include gradual start-up schedules that include home visiting, individual screening, or attendence of part of the class at a time. As a result, teachers have less time to observe, document, and collect information about students, and the amount of information teachers can collect must be adjusted to reflect decreased time with students.

This section will describe the differences in each of the three elements of the Work Sampling System.

Developmental Guidelines and Checklists

Completion of the Developmental Checklists does not differ in preschool classrooms. Preschool teachers tend to be very familiar with checklists and observational records and this part of the system fits easily into their classrooms. Using the Checklist tends to sharpen teachers' observation skills as they watch for behavior related to each performance indicator within the context of ongoing classroom activities. As recommended for elementary grades, teachers can begin to implement Work Sampling using only three or four of the domains, adding more throughout the year.

Portfolios

Although Portfolios at the preschool level have the same purposes as Portfolios for elementary-age children, the learning characteristics of three and four year olds necessitate changes in focus and methods of collection. Preschool children learn in very concrete ways. They must actively manipulate objects, and directly experience events and explore materials in order to learn about them. At this age, exploration is the centerpiece of children's learning. However, young children's explorations do not often culminate in the creation of products. Reflecting the unique charactersitics of learning during the preschool years, collections of preschoolers' work assumes a different character from Portfolios of older children.

Preschool Portfolio collection differs in three important ways from Portfolio collection with older children:

1 methods of documentation

2 collection of Core Items

3 the role of the child

DOCUMENTATION Preschool Portfolios document the *process* of learning and include fewer actual examples of the child's work. In order to document this process, teachers record "word pictures" of a child's participation in classroom activities. A preschool teacher might describe how a child interacts with objects, plays with other children, or moves around the classroom, as shown in Examples 1–3.

EXAMPLE 1   *While cutting the outer layer off a ball of playdough with a plastic knife, Mandy explained, "I'm making potatoes. I'm peeling them."*

EXAMPLE 2   *Exploring with the farm stamps, Luis says, "You press really hard, like this, and then you get a picture."*

EXAMPLE 3   *Taniesha picks up the tape measure, and measures the length of the 'Discovery Table.' "A mouse is this big," she says, as she pulls the tape about six inches. Taniesha then pulls the tape out "real long" to measure her friend Shaina.*

These records are entirely descriptive, without any interpretations or conclusions by the teacher. More than observational notes that support Checklist ratings, Portfolio observational records provide a description not only of what children can do, but of how they do it. They are almost like video clips that capture a moment in the child's classroom experience.

At the preschool level, evaluating growth over time remains a major objective of Portfolio collection. Progress can be demonstrated through documentation of the same areas of learning on repeated occasions. In the following example, the teacher defined a Core Item for Social Studies as, "The child's awareness and understanding of social roles as represented in dramatic play." The three records follow:

During the fall, Tom rarely entered the house corner, and seemed to prefer gross motor activities (running, climbing, etc.), fine motor materials (puzzles, Legos, writing), and the computer. He was not observed taking on a role in dramatic play.

In winter, the teacher made the following anecdotal record (Example 4):

EXAMPLE 4   *Tom was playing with 3 other children in the block area. They had made a "house" of blocks and were playing with the Duplo people. Steven said, "Grandma will sleep like this," putting one person in one room, "and the children will sleep in here," putting three people in another room.*

He made one person walk up to another on the wall and say, "We're off to New York!" and then he took both of them and made them fly around. He said, "Aaah . . . going to New York!" as they flew through the air. And "Aaah . . . we went to New York!" as they landed.

In spring, the anecdotal record reads (Example 5):

Tom was playing with the doctor's kit in the house area. He held a doll behind the x-ray machine and operated it. He stood the doll in front of the eye chart and recited A – Z (all of the alphabet is on the eye chart). Then he lifted the "hammer" to check reflexes and said, "Do it gently, now." He tapped the doll's knees and feet. Then he said, "Hmm. I think he needs a shot." Tom picked up the syringe, gave the doll a shot and said, "Owww!"

Together, these anecdotal records, Tom's fall, winter, and spring Core Items, demonstrate the growth Tom has made in his understanding of social roles in dramatic play.

Some other ways that teachers document learning include:

■ taking photographs of children at work and writing a narrative to describe the photo;

■ videotaping activities;

■ audiotaping children's language or singing; and

■ writing down dictations of stories or conversations.

Whether the teacher writes a "word picture," takes a photo, or audiotapes a conversation, the teacher's documentation becomes the Portfolio item. Although many Portfolio items will be teacher narratives or documentations, some of the child's work, such as art work, writing, cutting samples, and collages, can also be included. These products are natural outgrowths of the child's participation in classroom activities.

CORE ITEM COLLECTION In preschool classrooms, Core Items can be collected from Personal and Social Development and from Physical Development. These domains are so central to the preschool experience that many teachers believe that they should be made prominent in the Portfolio. Preschool teachers may decide to keep track of children's play interactions, independence, eye-hand coordination, or balance over the course of the year. If desired, preschool teachers may decide to eliminate two of the other domains, in order to keep the workload manageable. Examples of Core Items for preschoolers in all seven domains are listed in the Appendix.

ROLE OF THE CHILD A third characterisitc that distinguishes preschool Portfolio collection is the role of the child. Preschool children can review and reflect upon their activities and work, but very few preschool children can make judgments about the quality of their work and evaluate their progress over time. Therefore, the development of standards for school work as a goal and outcome of Portfolio collection is less relevant for preschool children than for older children.

It is important for preschoolers to know that their work is being saved and reproduced for their own Portfolio collections. Their Portfolios should be stored in a visible location, where they can look at them occasionally and share them with their families. They may want to save something they have made by including it in their Portfolio. Portfolios can become a vehicle for recalling school activities and beginning to appreciate growth over time.

Preschool children usually want to take their work home, even when they know about their Portfolio. Some ways that teachers have handled this issue are to:

- photocopy items for the Portfolios;

- keep one copy of a project — if the child has made two — for the Portfolio and send the other one home;

- put work on the bulletin board as an intermediary step before putting it in the child's portfolio; and

- send work home with a note asking the family to send it back for the Portfolio collection after they have discussed the work with their child.

It is important to remember that if a child of this age feels strongly about taking a particular sample of work home, the teacher should allow this. Children will create other examples that can be kept for their Portfolios.

Summary Reports

We do not recommend the use of report cards for preschool children, but we do encourage regular, systematic communication with families about their child's learning. The Work Sampling System has two different report forms: the standard Summary Report and the Narrative Summary Report. Some preschool teachers prefer to use the Narrative Summary Report because it more closely resembles narrative reports with which they are already familiar. Regardless of the choice of form, teachers summarize information from the Checklists and Portfolios at the end of each collection period, evaluate children's performance and progress, and address areas that will be emphasized during the next collection period.

Gradual Implementation in Preschool Classrooms

Preschool teachers may want to implement the System gradually during the first year. If so, they may begin with Checklist completion and Portfolio collection in three domains and add two more domains during each of the following collection periods. Other ways to reduce the workload while teachers are learning the system include: collecting only one Core

Item in each domain, collecting only three Individualized Items per collection period, or writing only two Summary Reports. However, after teachers are comfortable implementing Work Sampling, we encourage teachers to collect two Core Items per domain, five Individualized Items per collection period, and to complete three Summary Reports each school year. Because children grow so rapidly during the preschool years, three Summary Reports provide a more accurate portrait of children's growth.

Using Work Sampling to Assess Children with Special Needs

The Work Sampling System has been used successfully to assess children with special needs who are included in regular education classrooms. In fact, several features of the Work Sampling System make it particularly appropriate for the assessment of children with special needs. First, Work Sampling takes an individualized approach to learning and assessment. Children are not compared to one another, but are compared to standards of performance identified in the Developmental Guidelines. Moreover, because Work Sampling evaluates progress as well as performance, it allows children with special needs to demonstrate growth even in areas where their performance is delayed.

The Work Sampling System's emphasis on ongoing assessment embedded within the classroom curriculum is also particularly relevant for children with special needs, many of whom have difficulty performing "on demand." In order to obtain an accurate picture of their strengths and weaknesses, it is critical to observe them over time and in a variety of circumstances. The emphasis Work Sampling places on repeated observation of learning within the classroom context ensures a comprehensive picture of each child's typical behavior.

Work Sampling's focus on classroom-based assessment and the use of assessment information to inform instruction makes it very compatible with the Individual Educational Plans (IEPs) required for children with special needs. IEPs provide detailed assessments of the child's needs and equally detailed plans for instruction that are updated regularly. Work Sampling's individualized profile of each child's development created through extensive collection and observation of student work and behavior in seven domains is a very useful and powerful method for informing the IEP. In addition, Work Sampling assists teachers in planning appropriate and meaningful curricula that promote the movement of children toward their greatest potential.

Just as curricular adaptation may be necessary for a child with special needs to participate fully in learning activities, adaptations may also be needed in the Work Sampling System. The severity of a child's handicapping condition will be a major determinant of the necessary adaptations.

Developmental Guidelines and Checklists

As teachers use the Work Sampling System with children with special needs, they most often make adaptations to the Checklists. Modifications may include interpreting indicators in a more inclusive way, deleting indicators or components, and supplementing the Work Sampling System with other more specialized assessments.

In many places, it is possible to change the language of the performance indicators to encompass varied expressions of the indicator and the use of adaptive equipment. For example, in the domain of Language and Literacy, the first indicator under the Component of Speaking in first grade is "Speaks easily, conveying ideas in discussions and conversations." "Speaking" can be interpreted as communicating in order to reflect the fact that children with special needs may communicate in ways other than speaking (such as with gestures, signs, facial expressions, and communication boards). The language used in the Guidelines' indicators is designed to be inclusive so that a child's development can be noted even when a handicapping condition is present (for example, using the word "communicates" instead of "verbalizes"; and "notices" instead of "sees").

Sometimes particular indicators, components, or domains will assume greater importance for children with disabilities. For example, for children with physical impairments, learning how to ask for assistance and how to appropriately decline assistance are central to the development of independence. Similarly, the domain of Personal and Social Development assumes increased emphasis for children with behavioral or emotional disabilities.

Some components or performance indicators may not be appropriate for individual children and should be omitted. For example, most of the performance indicators in the Physical Development section may not be appropriate for children with moderate to severe cerebral palsy. These indicators would be omitted and replaced with more relevant performance indicators. A child with a moderate to severe mental impairment may require elimination of performance indicators requiring higher-level abstract thinking skills, such as "Makes logical predictions when pursuing scientific investigations" in Scientific Thinking.

Obviously, limitations apply to the applicability of Work Sampling for some children with disabilities. Given the variety of needs even among children with the same disability, no single assessment can address all needs. Children with special needs may require additional assessment in some areas. For example, a child with motoric involvement may require intervention to improve oral-motor ability in order to help the child speak more clearly. In that case, a performance indicator could be added to encompass the area of oral-motor control. Similarly, a severe visual impairment warrants the assessment of mobility. When development in a given domain is very different or delayed, a specialized instrument administered by a therapist or special education consultant may be necessary to supplement information obtained through Work Sampling. When a child's functioning is below that of a three year old, other assessments would be more effective and informative than the Work Sampling System.

Teachers frequently ask whether they should always use the Checklist that corresponds to a child's chronological age. This decision should be made in conjunction with family members and special education consultants. An important factor to consider is whether the child has a general developmental delay and is performing at a consistent level across the seven Work Sampling domains, or whether the child's performance varies widely from one domain to another. For example, if a child is experiencing a general developmental delay, using the grade level Checklist that corresponds to a child's chronological age may not be appropriate because all indicators would be rated "Not Yet." If all of the indicators are far beyond the child's current capabilities, then the Checklist would not demonstrate the child's progress, nor would it inform instructional planning. In such cases, it is more useful to use a Checklist that more nearly reflects the child's *developmental* age. In this way, the child's growth can be reflected as the year progresses.

In contrast, for children functioning near their age level in several domains, it may be most appropriate to use the Checklist that corresponds to their chronological age. This Checklist could be supplemented with additional assessments in areas of delay and with information from the Guidelines that describes younger children. However, it is important that teachers do not underestimate a child's capabilities by using a Checklist that most closely reflects the child's weakest area.

Portfolios

Portfolio collection provides specific information about how a child learns and works. It also provides a focus for discussion between a classroom teacher and other team members (for example, consultants, therapists, and psychologists). By documenting how the work was completed (noting adaptations, amount of help required), the teacher has valuable information to share with other team members who may have much less contact with the child.

Summary Reports

Teachers complete Summary Reports the same way for children with and without special needs. Some children with special needs will have a more uneven developmental profile and may show more frequent discrepancies between performance and progress. A child with a moderate degree of mental impairment may be delayed according to the Guidelines, but his progress may still be remarkable. When a child needs support in order to perform at a certain level, that information can be indicated on the Summary Report. For example, one might note "after brainstorming and discussing a story with a peer tutor, Susie is able to write a three-part story."

Working on a Team

We recommend that the classroom teacher collaborate with Special Education teachers and consultants. By using the child's Portfolio and Checklist, the teacher can communicate clearly with specialists and family members about how the child performs in the classroom. Because the classroom teacher is able to spend more time with the child, she has a wealth of specific knowledge about how the child approaches learning. The rich, detailed, individualized portraits that the Work Sampling System provides make it a valuable addition to the educational assessment of children with special needs.

Working with Specialists

The role of the special subject teacher in the Work Sampling System is dependent on how specialists are used in each district. Many aspects of this role vary depending on such factors as:

- whether the district employs specialists;

- which curriculum areas are taught by specialists;

- frequency and duration of the specialist's contact with students;

- size of the specialist's caseload; and

- whether the specialist is responsible for student evaluation

The determination of the appropriate role can only be made after consideration of the district and contractual realities that influence how specialists currently function.

Work Sampling is a method of classroom-based performance assessment that relies heavily on classroom teachers' expertise and professional judgment regarding student performance across all domains of learning.

We believe that each domain is an important and necessary curriculum area that can and should be addressed by classroom teachers. For this reason, the Guidelines and Checklists for The Arts and Physical Development are based on classroom teachers', not specialists', level of knowledge. These Guidelines and Checklists reflect the types of skills, performances, and accomplishments that teachers observe in the classroom. If circumstances within a district do not lend themselves to involving specialists in Work Sampling, teachers may evaluate those domains independently of the work of specialists.

A more effective solution to the relationship between classroom teachers and specialists lies in teacher/specialist collaboration. Both classroom teachers and specialists benefit from each other's expertise and their rich collaboration can take many forms. Optimally, the classroom teacher and the specialist will share their knowledge about students. Many specialists use their own skill-based inventories to meet their evaluation needs. When this information is shared with classroom teachers, Checklist ratings become more accurate as they reflect more detailed and comprehensive observations. However, specialists who see many children for short class periods find it difficult to collect and organize observations for Checklist ratings. Under these circumstances, it may be best for classroom teachers to discuss students' performance and progress with specialists before completing the Checklist and the Summary Report.

Depending on the time available for joint planning, teachers and specialists may also collaborate to plan activities that may result in items for the Portfolio. Sharing knowledge about a domain among classroom teachers and specialists may result in activities that are more in-depth and meaningful. Themes and investigations carried out in the classroom can be enriched by extension into special subject areas. Similarly, the content of activities in the special class can illuminate concepts presented in the classroom. We discourage classroom teachers from turning over Checklist sections or entire domains to the specialist for evaluation. Rather, to maximize the knowledge of specialists, we suggest that collaborative efforts be used to provide classroom teachers, specialists, and children with the richest possible experience.

The Special Subject Report form (see page 107) has been designed to facilitate communication between specialists and classroom teachers. This form lists all seven domains and allows special subject teachers to check the domains that they want to evaluate. They write brief narratives that include information for the classroom teacher. It is a four-part, carbonless form with copies for the classroom teacher, the special subject teacher, the family, and the school.

Using Work Sampling in Multi-age Classrooms

The Work Sampling System is very appropriate for multi-age classrooms. Many of these classrooms use Work Sampling as an assessment tool because of its emphasis on the continuum of children's development. By examining the six levels of an indicator presented in the Omnibus Guidelines, teachers can see what comes before and what comes after each indicator.

COMPLETING CHECKLISTS Although the Omnibus Guidelines present several levels of development at once, the Checklists do not. Teachers in multi-age groups will use several different Checklists to cover the ages represented by the students. Because all of the domains, most of the components, and many of the indicators are the same across several grade levels, teachers do not have to learn entirely new information for each grade represented in their classrooms. In the Guidelines, the rationales and examples distinguish between age levels. Teachers in multi-age classrooms complete different checklists, but refer to the Guidelines for developmental descriptions of the indicators.

USING PORTFOLIOS Multi-age teachers can use the same Core Items for all the students in their classrooms. Because areas of learning are defined broadly, multi-age teachers are able to select areas of learning that are relevant for all of the grades represented in their classroom. Although Portfolio collection is structured in the same way for all students, children are free to represent their learning in ways reflective of their own levels of development.

Informing the School Community

When a school or district decides to implement the Work Sampling System, informing the community about the need for change and the reasoning that culminated in the decision for change helps to ensure successful adoption. To understand the Work Sampling System and accept it, family members accustomed to graded report cards may require help to learn how students can be evaluated without grades. They need concrete information about the Work Sampling System, about the materials they will receive, about how these materials demonstrate their child's performance and progress, and about the role of the Work Sampling System in maintaining educational standards. It is important to explain to families why the school has decided to implement the Work Sampling System, and what the teachers and the principal perceive as the System's potential benefits. Family members need to be informed that the Work Sampling System Summary Report will take the place of traditional report cards.

It is helpful for schools to enlist the support of the community so that the Work Sampling System will be well received. As with families, community members should receive an introduction to the System and the materials, and an understanding of the school's reasons for adopting Work Sampling as their assessment system.

Some of the information that families need is provided in the OVERVIEW FOR FAMILIES, included in Work Sampling System Classroom Packs and Student Materials Packs. However, written information works best when combined with face-to-face interaction. We recommend that several opportunities be provided for family members to meet with the school principal/director and teachers. In order to make the transition as smooth as possible, we suggest that each program, school, or school district design and implement strategies for informing the families and the larger school community about the Work Sampling System. Components of informing the community about the Work Sampling System include:

1 Scheduling a series of parent meetings led by teachers and the principal or director

2 Sending a personalized letter home with the Overview for Families.

3 Assigning the principal or other staff member to respond to parents' questions and concerns.

4 Informing the Parent Teacher Organization and involving PTO members in planning an outreach campaign (such as visits to local service organizations, newspaper articles, and radio spots).

5 Inviting families and community members to an open house, to provide contact with teachers and an introduction to Portfolio Collection.

6 Making a presentation to the school or community board or other public forum.

7 Conducting family-teacher conferences at the end of the first collection period.

8 Creating and distributing question and answer brochures about the Work Sampling System and its relationship to local concerns.

Case Study

One school used the following strategies to inform the community about the Work Sampling System:

1 Sent a letter home with the Overview for Families. Early in September, the principal and volunteer teachers drafted a letter to send home. The letter explained that the school would be using a new system to evaluate students, described the system briefly, and discussed why the school decided to try it. Families received a letter signed by all members of the team (principal, classroom teachers, specialist teachers, and special education staff) along with a copy of the Overview for Families.

At the end of the letter, a form asked parents to describe their need for further information. Family members could indicate if they felt they had sufficient information about the Work Sampling System; if they wanted more written information about the system; if they wanted to attend a meeting with other parents and school staff to discuss the system further; or if they would like to meet with their child's classroom teacher.

2 Assigned the principal or other staff member to respond to parents' questions and concerns. The principal was available to respond to families when they called to ask for more information or to comment on the initial letter and the Overview for Families.

3 Informed the Parent Teacher Organization and involved PTO members in planning an outreach campaign. From the beginning, parents played an integral role in this campaign. A group of parents attended informational meetings about Work Sampling so that they could be a resource for other parents. They assisted school staff in writing the letter, and planning the parent meeting, open house, and the presentation to the School Board. Members of the parent organization discussed the Work Sampling System with other parents and related parents' responses and concerns to school staff.

4 Scheduled a parent meeting led by teachers and principal. In late September, in response to parent preferences, school staff scheduled parent meetings at two different times of the day to accommodate parents' varying schedules. Both the principal and the teachers attended the meeting. They displayed Work Sampling System materials for parents to review, gave an overview and explanation of the System, answered questions, and discussed why they welcomed the change.

5 Invited families and community members to an Open House, to provide contact with teachers and an introduction to Portfolio Collection. This school holds an Open House at the beginning of each school year. Part of this event involves gathering parents from each class to meet their child's teacher and see the classroom. Teachers devoted a portion of this meeting specifically to discussing the Work Sampling System. They showed family members where Portfolios were kept, and described the process of collecting work to include in the Portfolio.

6 **Made a presentation to the School Board.** In this school district, School Board meetings are open to the public and are generally well-attended. In early October, the principal and a few of the teachers prepared a presentation for the School Board. The principal described the components of the Work Sampling System and the steps that had been taken in the school to inform families about the new assessment system. Teachers explained how assessment takes place in the classroom. They described the process of observation for Checklist evaluation and the involvement of children in Portfolio collection. Staff also presented their reasons for implementing Work Sampling in their school.

7 **Held family-teacher conferences at the end of the first collection period.** At the end of the first collection period, family-teacher conferences were scheduled. The teachers devoted much of the first conference to introducing the components of Work Sampling, and answering any questions raised by family members. Teachers showed family members their child's Portfolio and discussed her/his knowledge, skills, and progress in the classroom. Teachers and family members discussed the Summary Report, and made plans to support the child's growth. At the end of the conference, parents received a copy of the Summary Report.

Teachers used the Portfolio to focus the discussion of student work and accomplishments during the family-teacher conference. They informed the child's family about the developmental progression in children's work and the developmental standards to which children are held when teachers use the Work Sampling System. With teacher guidance, family members can learn to recognize their child's strengths, weaknesses, and progress in the work included in the Portfolio. Teachers at this school spoke about how crucial it was to present the system to parents as thoroughly and positively as possible. In the end, they also found that children's work speaks for itself. In fact, children are the best ambassadors for the Work Sampling System. At events such as Portfolio Night (see page 79), children present their work to their families and reflect upon it with them. When teachers, students, and families are involved in the process of assessment, the resulting information is comprehensive and better supports children's growth.

CHAPTER 6

Helpful Ideas for Getting Organized

HAVING READ THIS MANUAL, YOU MAY FIND IT HELPFUL TO REVIEW what you need to do to get started using the Work Sampling System. The first part of this chapter identifies several steps and directs you to the appropriate section of this manual to find additional information about each topic. The second section of this chapter reminds teachers of two issues essential to the successful implementation of the Work Sampling System: informing the community and collaborating with colleagues. Following that section is a list of suggestions for weekly planning. Finally, the last section addresses the teacher as learner, and strategies for supporting the teacher in this new effort.

Steps for Getting Started

1 **Read and familiarize yourself with the Developmental Guidelines.** (see page 17).

2 **Set up your Portfolio collection system.** Decide what kind of system you will use to collect children's work. Label individual Portfolios with children's names. Put domain labels on files. Determine how and where to store Portfolios (see page 48).

3 **Plan Core Items with other teachers in your building or district.** Complete the Core Item Collection Plan master. Make a copy for each child's Portfolio (see page 60).

4 **Set up work folders for each child to use as "holding" bins for their work before items are chosen for the Portfolio.** Determine where they should be placed in the classroom (see page 50). Post-It™ notes should be available nearby for the child and you to comment about the work and its reason for inclusion.

5 **Set up an organizational system for observation and Checklist review.** This working file stores the Checklist, notes and reminders about activities to observe or plan, observation notes, correspondence with the family, and any other materials about children that will help you with their evaluations (see page 18).

6 **Decide on a system for documenting observations of children.** Are any of the Checklist Process Notes be useful to you? If you think of another way to keep track of your observations, design a master. Make

enough copies of your process note sheets to use during the first weeks of school. Fill in the children's names as appropriate (see page 20).

7 Develop a plan for ongoing observation. Plan how, when, and what you will observe during the first days and weeks of school (see page 19).

8 Consider how to involve children in the assessment process. Decide on a way to introduce Portfolios and work folders to children. Think about whether you are ready to involve students in work collection and review (see page 74). If so, how will you introduce these activities to your students? Consider ways to let students know how and why you observe them (see page 40).

Ensuring a Smooth Start

Because schools are parts of larger communities, teachers find it helpful to do the following:

■ **Inform parents about the Work Sampling System.** If this has not already been done the previous spring, make a plan for activities to inform families and the larger community about the Work Sampling System (see pages 123 – 126).

■ **Set up a regular schedule with colleagues for follow-up planning and support.** The first year of using Work Sampling is a year of change. Discussion with colleagues on a regular basis supports the processes of reflection and implementation. We recommend scheduling staff development sessions every two to five weeks. These discussions can be used to:

- discuss progress and problems encountered,

- plan for events to come (such as a "Portfolio Night"), and

- share ideas, management techniques, and successful solutions to problems.

Teachers can give each other enormous support and strategies for implementation if there is time for them to plan together and support each other as they make changes in the assessment process.

On a Weekly Basis

Teachers become comfortable using the Work Sampling System when it is integrated into their daily classroom routines. Taking 10 minutes of your planning time to schedule some of the activities associated with Work Sampling will facilitate your effective use of the System. Consider the following:

1 Review the activities that you have planned for the week; highlight those activities that may result in the creation of Core Items.

2 Think about how well your systems of observation and documentation are working for you; make changes that you can try during the following week.

3 Schedule time for observation; plan how, what, and when you will observe.

4 Schedule regular time to do the management tasks associated with this assessment process, such as record keeping and filing.

Timeline

The timeline illustration below suggests an approximate time-frame for the activities associated with the Checklist, Portfolio, and Summary Report during a single collection period.

	PREPARATION	COLLECTION PERIOD BEGINS								COLLECTION PERIOD ENDS	REPORTING PERIOD ENDS
GUIDELINES & CHECKLISTS		Week 1	Week 2	Week 3	Week 4	Week 5	Week 6	Week 7	Week 8	Week 9	Week 10	Week 11

GUIDELINES & CHECKLISTS

Set-up observation records & Checklist storage

Observe & Record (Weeks 1–3)
Observe & Record (Weeks 5–6)
Observe & Record (Week 8)

Review & Rate (Preliminary)
Review & Rate (Preliminary)
Review & Rate (Final)

	Week 1	Week 2	Week 3	Week 4	Week 5	Week 6	Week 7	Week 8	Week 9	Week 10	Week 11

PORTFOLIO COLLECTION

Prepare Portfolios, work folders, & Portfolio storage

Collect / Collect / Collect / Collect / Collect / Collect

Review & Select / Review & Select / Review & Select / Review & Select / Review & Select / Review & Select

Student review & evaluation of Portfolios, if appropriate

Final Portfolio Selection

	Week 1	Week 2	Week 3	Week 4	Week 5	Week 6	Week 7	Week 8	Week 9	Week 10	Week 11

SUMMARY REPORT

Complete Summary Report
Student review of Summary Report & goal setting, if appropriate

AFTERWARDS
Summary Report Sent Home & Conference Held

Tips for Teachers as They Learn Work Sampling

"Be Patient, Be Flexible, Have Faith, and Be Willing to Take Risks."

- It is not possible to do everything at once.

- It is not possible to become knowledgeable about something new without going through a period of learning.

- Learning includes trial and error, making mistakes, and growing.

- Learning may be uncomfortable, and requires patience and time.

- Learning happens best when there is "hands-on" experience and time for "messing about."

Teachers believe all of the above statements when describing the learning environment they set up for students. Allow *yourself* the same optimal learning conditions when embarking on the implementation of the Work Sampling System.

The first year of learning Work Sampling can feel daunting. It is important to be flexible and allow yourself time to become familiar with the System. Remember that Work Sampling is intended to work for you. Try to use Work Sampling in a way that fits your classroom life, your curriculum, and your personal approach to learning and work. One way to help you manage implementation is to focus on the goal of each activity. For example, when writing the commentary for Summary Reports, think about what is essential to communicate to families, and then organize yourself to address that goal. Approaching Work Sampling in this way will help you to maintain reasonable expectations of yourself as you learn to implement the System.

There are several comfortable ways to implement Work Sampling gradually over the course of a school year. Suggestions include:

- During the Fall collection period, address only the first three domains for both Checklists and Portfolio collection. Then, the fall Summary Report will reflect only these three domains. During your first winter collection period, add two more domains using both Checklists and Portfolio Collection. Your winter Summary Reports will include information in these five domains. Finally, include all seven domains in your spring collection.

— *or* —

- For the entire first year, only do three domains in their entirety. Use information from the Guidelines to guide your understanding of the other domains but do not demand of yourself that Checklists and Portfolio collection be complete in the other four domains.

— *or* —

■ Complete Checklists for all domains but collect only one Core Item in each of the five domains for the first two collection periods and only two or three Individualized Items.

When teachers have time to prepare materials before the start of the school year and to establish methods for observation, documentation, and selection of student work, their initial attempts to use Work Sampling will be more successful. By informing the community about the change in assessment, and arranging for ongoing staff development opportunities, teachers further ensure successful adoption of the System. Most importantly, when teachers give themselves the same optimal conditions for learning that they try to provide for their students, their learning will more likely be successful and they will be on the way to full implementation of the Work Sampling System.

APPENDIX A

Suggestions for Core Items — Elementary

Language and Literacy

Area of Learning	Child's Work/Representation
1 Using writing to express ideas.	Stories, journal entries, scripts, poetry, fables, lists, signs for block buildings, articles for the class or school newspaper, reports, letters (written or dictated to a teacher).
2 Comprehending and interpreting literature.	A book report, illustration with dictation, photograph of a diorama, a rewritten ending to a story, story written in the style of the author, story mapping, letter to the author, or poster.
3 Using language to obtain information.	A child's record of interview questions they write and ask (e.g., for a visitor to the classroom), description of the process a child uses to investigate a topic (books a child read, a listing of sources used, etc.).
4 Using expressive language.	A drawing accompanied by text (dictated to a teacher or written by the child), a child's answers to interview questions posed by another child or the teacher, poems, essays, audio-tape of class debate or oral presentation.
5 Using strategies to read (emergent or conventional reading).	Audiotape or videotape of child reading aloud, a miscue analysis, a running reading record (e.g., letter-sound correspondence, use of sight words, using pictures to construct the story line, use of contextual cues, application of prior knowledge).

Mathematical Thinking

Area of Learning	Child's Work/Representation
1 Solving problems involving number.	Anecdotal record, audiotape, or videotape of a young child's counting, a young child's recording of the symbolic name for a quantity, an older child's solution to a word problem, or the writing of a word problem to go with a number sentence.
2 Understanding of matching, sorting, and classifying.	Picture/drawing/diagram or written description.
3 Solving problems involving estimating, calculating, and/or measuring.	Picture/drawing/diagram or written description.
4 Understanding of patterning and seriating.	Picture/drawing/diagram or written description.

Scientific Thinking

Area of Learning	Child's Work/Representation
1 Observing and recording scientific phenomena with accuracy.	Pictures, written descriptions, dictations
2 Collecting data about change over time.	Charts or graphs, written or dictated text, illustrations
3 Using scientific processes for investigation (questioning, predicting, applying knowledge, experimenting, drawing conclusions, generalizing, explaining, using tools).	Posters, drawings, reports, maps, graphs, charts, displays, oral presentations, etc.

Social Studies

Area of Learning	Child's Work/Representation
1 Understanding their neighborhood.	Photograph of a child's block building, a model, a story about a character from another culture, a diorama, a report about houses in different lands.
2 Understanding personal and family life (family roles, neighborhood, country of origin, etc.).	Written text, drawings, models, a life book (child gathers information about each year of his/her life and contributes to it throughout the school year).
3 Understanding another city, or region.	Drawing, research report, concept map.
4 Understanding of the interdependence of people's roles in the family and community.	Photograph, anecdotal records, written stories, paintings, portraits of themselves and family members, dictations or written descriptions of family roles, drawings of family members and their occupational roles.
5 Understanding of human similarities and differences.	A collage of different people, families, workers, cultures; written or dictated discussion of human similarities and differences, pictures, reports.

The Arts

Area of Learning	Child's Work/Representation
1 Using artistic media to express ideas or emotions.	Paintings, sculptures, collages, photographs taken by the child, etc.
2 Exploring and controlling an artistic medium.	Drawings in crayons, markers, chalk, or other media; paintings in watercolors, tempera, or other paint media; collages, three-dimensional or flat, in paper or other media; sculptures in clay, plaster, playdough or other sculpture media.
3 Responding to an experience involving the arts.	Writings about personal reactions to music, art, drama, dance; writing about the child's interpretation to a piece of music, drawing that expresses how an artistic experience made the child feel.
4 Singing, dancing, or playing an instrument.	Audiotapes, videotapes.

APPENDIX B

Suggestions for Core Items — Preschool

Language and Literacy

Area of Learning	Child's Work/Representation
1 Understanding and response to a story.	Drawings, dictations, retellings of the story (dictated or audio-taped).
2 Using verbal language to describe an event, classroom experience, or field trip.	Dictations, audio tapes.
3 Creating an original story.	Dictations, audio tapes.
4 Showing interest in reading-related activities.	Drawings, dictations, audio tapes, notes of conversation with another child, description of reading activity in the book corner.
5 Using emergent writing.	Journal entries, writing samples.

Mathematical Thinking

Area of Learning	Child's Work/Representation
1 Understanding of patterning.	Photos of work with manipulatives, paper replicates of created patterns.
2 Understanding of sorting by one or two attributes.	Photos, anecdotal records, collages.
3 Understanding of concepts of size.	Photos, anecdotal records, collages, dictation of comments or questions, child's contribution to class brainstorming chart.
4 Counting using one-to-one correspondence.	Photos, anecdotal records.

Scientific Thinking

Area of Learning	Child's Work/Representation
1 Solving problems during exploration.	Notes or photos taken during water or sand play.
2 Exploring and observing the natural world.	Notes or photos taken during water or sand play; records of comments or questions asked about scientific phenomena; dictation.
3 Predicting or guessing what will happen next.	Anecdotal notes, dictation, child's contribution to class list of suggestions for what will happen next.
4 Forming explanations of observations or explorations.	Dictation, anecdotal notes, audio tapes of exploration, record of an interview about a scientific experience.

Social Studies

Area of Learning	Child's Work/Representation
1 Recognizing own physical characteristics.	Verbal comments about the topic written down by the teacher, self portraits.
2 Recognizing family roles.	Notes or photos of a child's role-playing in blocks, outdoors, housekeeping or dramatic play, puppet play.
3 Showing awareness of community workers and their roles.	Photo of dramatic play, dictated comments after hearing a story about community workers, dictation after a field trip.

The Arts

Area of Learning	Child's Work/Representation
1 Exploring different art media.	Collages; drawings in crayons, markers, chalk; paintings in tempera, watercolor, fingerpaint; photos of clay or playdough creations.
2 Participating in visual arts, music, drama, or dance.	Audio tape of singing or playing instruments; videotape of creative dance, puppet show, play; artwork.
3 Exploring with a single medium.	Easel paintings, drawings with markers, drawings with crayons, collage, watercolor paintings.
4 Using art or drawing tools.	Brush work, drawings, printings, cuttings.

APPENDIX C

Example of Teacher's Letter to Parents

Here is the complete text of a first/second grade teacher's letter to families, sent home with the Summary Report.

" Dear _____

Along with this letter, you will find your child's Summary Report for the collection period. I'll try to give you an idea about the topics we've studied and activities children have participated in so you will have a clearer picture of your child's school experience. I'll use the seven Work Sampling domains to organize this information.

Personal and Social Development
We strive to create an environment in which children have ample opportunity to be active, independent learners as well as responsible members of the classroom community. Your child's report will give an indication of how she/he feels about her/himself as a learner and as a friend to others. It will also tell you about the nature of your child's learning style, social skills, and response to being in a group.

Language and Literacy
In this part of the Summary Report I offer a description of your child in the world of oral and written language. In our classroom, there is an emphasis on children's participation in group discussions. During this period, we've had discussions about fairness on the playground, problems and solutions in stories, things we know about clocks, reasons why scientists might go to a jungle, and ways we can help a new student feel comfortable in our class, just to name a few. I try to give you a sense of your child's role in these discussions, both as a listener and as a vocal participant.

There are a variety of opportunities for children to engage in reading during each day; some are informal and unstructured, while others are focused and instructional. Many different types and levels of books are available in the room. I'll give you information related to your child's attitude, interest level, attention span, and strategies related to various reading activities, as well as the kinds of books she/he reads.

Writing is also a daily activity in our classroom. The information you receive will relate to aspects of your child as an author and speller — attitude and interest in writing, the length and character of stories, and the developing accuracy of spelling.

Mathematical Thinking

Some aspects of the mathematics curriculum are ongoing throughout the year. Each Summary Report will shed light on the character, quality, and progress of your child's approach to solving different kinds of mathematical problems. During this period, many math problems related to double-digit numbers and shapes. We used a variety of materials to help solve problems - Cuisenaire Rods, unifix cubes, pattern blocks, and tangrams. Information in the Summary Report will characterize your child's approach to mathematical problems, her/his persistence level, and the degree of difficulty of the problems. During this period, we also did some activities about telling time, measuring, and graphing.

Scientific Thinking

In this domain, our curriculum emphasizes qualities and skills that can be applied to many topics of study. In this Summary Report you will read about your child's engagement with our study of the jungle habitat, as well as our ongoing involvement with the natural surroundings of the school. You will have a sense of your child's interest in and curiosity about the topic, a picture of your child as an observer and investigator, and a description about how your child applies and uses scientific information.

Social Studies

The Social Studies curriculum places an emphasis on children's growing understanding of people and the world. In our studies of different habitats, we tried to learn what people need in order to survive and how different environments affect the people who live, work, or visit there. This report will give you some information about your child's ability to understand and imagine living styles in different parts of the world.

The Arts

The curriculum in our classroom engages children in a variety of expressive activities as means by which they can share and integrate what they know. For example, music, drama, puppetry, dance, drawing, painting, sculpting, inventing, and building are some of the ways children might have represented their knowledge of predator/prey relationships in the jungle during this period. Your child's report describes her/his preferences of expressive avenues and the qualities of her/his creative endeavors. Other comments may shed light on your child's responses to the artistic endeavors of others, like a band concert given by older students.

Physical Development

An underlying belief of our classroom curriculum is that healthy physical development and an awareness of personal health and safety issues is critical to successful academic progress. The Summary Report will describe characteristics of both your child's gross motor and fine motor movements, as well as her/his level of self confidence in these areas.

After you have read and digested your child's report, I would encourage you to read and share it with your child. Little, if anything, should be a surprise to your child and she/he has a right to know what is being communicated between home and school. Here are a few generic questions you could ask as you go along in an effort to engage your child in conversation about the report:

• What else can you tell me about that?

• Can you give me an example of what the teacher is talking about?

• Tell me about a time when you became excited (frustrated, scared, happy, proud, sad, nervous) at school.

• What do you think would help you with this problem at school?

• Why do you think the teacher thinks you are such a good scientist (problem-solver, reader, friend)?

• Did the teacher forget to tell me anything you think is important?

I hope this letter has helped you gain a thorough picture of your child at school. Please feel free to call me or write a note if you still have any questions, comments, or concerns. ❞

— *Charlotte Stetson*

Brattleboro, VT

APPENDIX D

Glossary of Terms

Here is a guide to the vocabulary of Work Sampling.

As Expected — a progress rating on the Summary Report that indicates that the child has grown appropriately according to the teacher's professional judgment and knowledge of child development.

Checklist — *see Developmental Checklist*

Checklist Ratings — *see In Process, Not Yet, Proficient*

Collection Period — a duration of time during which data are collected in an ongoing manner in order to make an evaluation. Work Sampling has three collection periods: fall, winter, and spring.

Component — *see Functional Component*

Core Items — Representation of a particular area of learning within a domain. Collected from five domains three times a year, Core Items are designed to display both the quality of children's work and their progress in domain-related knowledge and skills.

Curriculum-embedded — an assessment that uses students' actual performance in the regular classroom routine as the "data" for evaluation.

Criterion-referenced — an assessment that evaluates a student's work with reference to specific criteria rather than with reference to other students' work.

Developing as Expected — a performance rating on the Summary Report that indicates that the child's performance meets or exceeds age- or grade-level expectations as identified in the Developmental Guidelines.

Developmental Checklist — a list of performance indicators for each grade level that are organized by curriculum domains and are used to collect, organize, and record teachers' observations.

Developmental Guidelines — a book that describes age- or grade-level expectations for the performance indicators; contains a rationale and examples for each indicator.

Domain — a broad area of the curriculum.

Examples — descriptions of ways that children demonstrate what they know and can do related to each performance indicator in the Developmental Guidelines.

Functional Component — a subset of a domain comprised of several performance indicators.

Guidelines — *see Developmental Guidelines*

Indicator — *see Performance Indicator*

Individualized Items — Portfolio items that capture the child's unique interests and experiences, and reflect learning that integrates many domains of the curriculum.

In Process — a Checklist rating that indicates that the skill or knowledge represented by a performance indicator is intermittent or emergent, and is not demonstrated consistently.

Needs Development — a performance rating on the Summary Report that indicates that the child's current performance does not meet age- or grade-level expectations.

Not Yet — a Checklist rating that indicates that a child cannot demonstrate the skill or knowledge represented by a performance indicator.

Omnibus Guidelines — two volumes (P3–3, K–5) that each display six years of Developmental Guidelines on facing pages, arranged to show year-to-year progress.

Other than Expected — a progress rating on the Summary Report that indicates that a child's progress is either above or below teacher expectations.

Performance — refers to the level of a student's behavior, skills, and accomplishments at a particular point in time.

Performance Assessment — refers to assessment methods that rely on students demonstrating their knowledge or skills in applied situations.

Performance Indicator — a skill, behavior, attitude, or accomplishment that is evaluated in the classroom.

Proficient — a Checklist rating that indicates that the skill or knowledge represented by a performance indicator is demonstrated consistently, and is firmly within the child's repertoire.

Progress — growth over time.

Portfolio — purposeful collection of children's work.

Rationale — a brief explanation of an indicator that includes reasonable age- or grade-level expectations.

Summary Report — a report completed three times during the school year that integrates information from the Developmental Checklist and Portfolio with teachers' knowledge of child development in order to evaluate a student's performance and progress.

Summary Report Performance Ratings — see *Developing as Expected, Needs Development*

Summary Report Progress Ratings — see *As Expected, Other than Expected*

Acknowledgements

THIS MANUAL REPRESENTS MORE THAN THREE YEARS' EXPERIENCE IN developing, implementing, and teaching the Work Sampling System. We are grateful to a large number of individuals for their contributions to this effort. At the risk of overlooking some, we wish to mention a few of the people we have relied on.

We thank the following colleagues for their valuable suggestions and feedback on an early draft: Lauren Ashley, Pam Becker, and Charlotte Stetson of the Brattleboro (VT) Public Schools; Joni Block and Laura Ruhkala of the Massachusetts Department of Education; Lucy Ware, from the Pittsburgh Public Schools; Austine Fowler, from the District of Columbia Public Schools.

Many teachers have contributed ideas, examples, and illustrations for this manual. From Brattleboro (VT) Public Schools: Jean Allbee, Pattie Berger, Deborah Hall, Janis Kiehle, Lynn Leighton, Polly Kurty, and Donna Natowich; From Pittsburgh Public Schools: Barbara Prevost; From Dexter (MI) Community Schools: Becky Wolfinger; From Flint (MI) Community Schools: Penny Butler; From Van Buren (MI) Public Schools: Cindy Israel and Melinda Mannes; From Massachusetts Project Impact: Jan Van Gieson, Barbara Moody, and Amy Rugel; From Carnegie Mellon University Child Care Center: Marsha Poster and Joella Reed; From Esteyville Preschool in Brattleboro (VT): David Bleecker-Adams, Jan Bucossi, and Joy Hammond.

Teachers and staff from the following districts shared their implementation experiences with us: Massachusetts districts of Agawam, Boston, Cambridge, Lynn, Old Rochester Regional School District, Pioneer Valley, and Somerset, and Lynn Economic Opportunity Head Start; Three schools affiliated with the Bureau of Indian Affairs: Canoncito, Chuska, Takini; Davison (MI) Community Schools; Dexter (MI) Community Schools; Flint (MI) Community Schools; Northview (MI) Public Schools; Van Buren (MI) Public Schools; Willow Run (MI) Community Schools; Pittsburgh Public Schools; Carnegie Mellon University Child Care Center; Fort Worth Independent School District; Brattleboro Public Schools; and the Valeska Hinton Early Childhood Center, Peoria, IL.

Others without whom the work could not have taken place include Jan Blomberg, Sue Kelley, Sally Atkins-Burnett, Pat McMahon, and Dorothy Steele for her contributions to the original formulation of the Work Sampling System. A special thanks to Donna Bickel whose readiness to consider a problem, answer questions, and share her experience was invaluable. Finally, we offer appreciation and thanks to

Tiff Crutchfield of Mode Design whose æsthetic sense and knowledge of the Work Sampling System enrich our work every step of the way.

This work was supported in part by a grant from the John D. and Catherine T. MacArthur Foundation awarded to Samuel J. Meisels, School of Education, University of Michigan. The opinions expressed are solely those of the authors.

— *Margo Dichtelmiller*
Judy Jablon
Aviva Dorfman
Dot Marsden
Sam Meisels